Fodor's 96
Pocket New
York City

Holida

D0449760

800 77 7392

X 5

SAHEIE

Reprinted from *Fodor's New York City '96*

Fodor's Travel Publications, Inc.
New York • Toronto • London • Sydney • Auckland

Fodor's Pocket New York City '96

Editors: Christopher Billy and Rebecca Miller
Editorial Contributors: Steven K. Amsterdam, Rob Andrews, Andrew Collins, Karen Cure, Stephanie Dolgoff, Theodore Fischer, Dick Kagan, Laura M. Kidder, David Low, Margaret Mittelbach, Marcy Pritchard, M. T. Schwartzman, Kate Sekules, Dinah Spritzer, J. Walman.
Creative Director: Fabrizio La Rocca
Cartographer: David Lindroth
Cover Photograph: Paul Chesley/Photographers/Aspen
Text Design: Between the Covers

Copyright

Special Sales

Fodor's Travel Publications are available at special discounts for bulk purchases for sales promotions or premiums. Special editions, including personalized covers, excerpts of existing guides, and corporate imprints, can be created in large quantities for special needs. For more information, contact your local bookseller or write to Special Markets, Fodor's Travel Publications, 201 East 50th Street, New York, NY 10022. Inquiries from Canada should be directed to your local Canadian bookseller or sent to Random House of Canada, Ltd., Marketing Department, 1265 Aerowood Drive, Mississauga, Ontario L4W 1B9. Inquiries from the United Kingdom should be sent to Fodor's Travel Publications, 20 Vauxhall Bridge Road, London SW1V 2SA.

MANUFACTURED IN THE UNITED STATES OF AMERICA
10 9 8 7 6 5 4 3 2 1

CONTENTS

Maps

ON THE ROAD WITH FODOR'S

A **GOOD TRAVEL GUIDE** is like a wonderful traveling companion. It's charming, it's brimming with sound recommendations and solid ideas, it pulls no punches in describing lodging and dining establishments, and it's consistently full of fascinating facts that make you view what you've traveled to see in a rich new light. In the creation of *Pocket New York City '96*, we at Fodor's have gone to great lengths to provide you with the very best of all possible traveling companions—and to make your trip the best of all possible vacations.

What's New

Big things are happening at Fodor's—and in New York City.

A New Design

If this is not the first Fodor's guide you've purchased, you'll immediately notice our new look. More readable and easier to use than ever? We think so—and we hope you do, too.

Let Us Do Your Booking

Our writers have scoured New York City to come up with an extensive and well-balanced list of the best B&Bs, inns, and hotels, both small and large, new and old. But you don't have to beat the bushes to come up with a reservation. Now we've teamed up with an established hotel-booking service to make it easy for you to secure a room at the property of your choice. It's fast, it's free, and confirmation is guaranteed. If your first choice is booked, the operators can line up your second right away. Just call 800/FODORS–1 or 800/363–6771 (0800/89–1030 when in Great Britain; 0014/800–12–8271 when in Australia; 1800/55–9109 when in Ireland).

And in New York City

The most exciting development/revitalization project in the city is happening in Chelsea. The **Chelsea Piers,** a 1.2-million-square-foot sports and entertainment complex on the Hudson River opened the first of its facilities in the summer of 1995. Officially launched in 1994, the $60-million, privately financed project is transforming four historic but long-neglected piers into a major center for public recreation and waterfront access. Once the berth of some of the world's great ocean liners, the renovated piers—between 17th and 24th streets—are now a bustling port of call for athletes, tourists, shoppers, and restaurant goers.

The first national museum dedicated to Native American culture opened in Manhattan last year. The **National Museum of the American Indian,** housed in the Alexander Hamilton Custom House at Bowling Green, examines the current cultures of native peoples from the Americas.

There were four major openings on the dining front in 1995: the incredibly beautiful **American Renaissance** in the American Thread Building in TriBeCa; **Aja,** at Broadway and 22nd, with its fantastic decor and futuristic mix of new American, Southwestern, Asian, and classic French cuisines; **Nobu** (also in TriBeCa), named for master chef Nobu Matsuhisa, whose Los Angeles restaurant has long been considered the best Japanese restaurant in America; and last but not least, **Bryant Park Grill,** which burst onto the scene with considerable fanfare. Supported by the Bryant Park Restoration Corporation, the New York Public Library, and the New York Parks Department, it is situated behind the library in recently restored and relandscaped Bryant Park. Diners can opt for the more casual Bryant Park Café on the rooftop, which has its own very charming garden and offers a serene view of the park.

How to Use this Guide

Organization

Up front is the **Essential Information** chapter chock-full of information about traveling within your destination and traveling in general. **Important Contacts** gives addresses and telephone numbers of organizations and companies that offer destination-related services and detailed information or publications. Here's where you'll find information about how to get to New York City from wherever you are. **Smart Travel Tips,** the Essential Information's second section, gives specific tips on how to get the most out of your travels, as well as information on how to accomplish what you need to in New York.

Stars

Stars in the margin are used to denote highly recommended sights, attractions, hotels, and restaurants.

Credit Cards

The following abbreviations are used: **AE,** American Express; **D,** Discover; **DC,** Diners Club; **MC,** MasterCard; and **V,** Visa.

Please Write to Us

Everyone who has contributed to *Fodor's Pocket New York City '96* has worked hard to make the text accurate. All prices and opening times are based on information supplied to us at press time, and Fodor's cannot accept responsibility for any errors that may have occurred. The passage of time will bring changes, so it's always a good idea to call ahead and confirm information when it matters—particularly if you're making a detour to visit specific sights or attractions. When making reservations at a hotel or inn, be sure to speak up if you have a disability or are traveling with children, if you prefer a private bath or a certain type of bed, or if you have specific dietary needs or any other concerns.

Were the restaurants we recommended as described? Did our hotel picks exceed your expectations? Did you find a museum we recommended a waste of time? We would love your feedback, positive and negative. If you have complaints, we'll look into them and revise our entries when the facts warrant it. If you've happened upon a special place that we haven't included, we'll pass the information along to the writers so they can check it out. So please send us a letter or postcard (we're at 201 East 50th Street, New York, New York 10022.) We'll look forward to hearing from you. And in the meantime, have a wonderful trip!

Karen Cure
Editorial Director

Manhattan Neighborhoods

HARLEM

Morningside Park

Marcus Garvey Park

W. 116th St.

E. 116th St.

Randall's Island

Henry Hudson Pkwy.

E. 110th St.

Riverside Drive

Broadway

Amsterdam Ave.

Columbus Ave.

Central Park West

Central Park

Ward's Island

W. 96th St.

E. 96th St.

UPPER WEST SIDE

UPPER EAST SIDE

W. 86th St.

E. 86th St.

West End Ave.

E. 79th St.

Park Ave.

QUEENS

W. 72nd St.

E. 72nd St.

Roosevelt Island

Broadway

E. 65th St.

E. 59th St.

FDR Dr.

Queensboro Bridge

W. 57th St.

E. 57th St.

11th Ave.

10th Ave.

9th Ave.

8th Ave.

5th Ave.

3rd Ave.

1st Ave.

Ave.

Queens-Midtown Tunnel

Lincoln Tunnel

W. 42nd St.

E. 42nd St.

MIDTOWN

Madison Ave.

Lexington Ave.

2nd Ave.

East River

W. 34th St.

7th Ave.

of the Americas

Broadway

W. 23rd St.

E. 23rd St.

CHELSEA

W. 14th St.

GRAMERCY

E. 14th St.

GREENWICH VILLAGE

West St.

EAST VILLAGE

W. Houston St.

E. Houston St.

Williamsburg Bridge

SOHO

Broadway

LITTLE ITALY

Canal St.

CHINA TOWN

Holland Tunnel

TRIBECA

Chambers St.

Manhattan Bridge

Hudson River

Brooklyn Bridge

N

LOWER MANHATTAN

BROOKLYN

Battery Park

Brooklyn-Battery Tunnel

Manhattan Subways

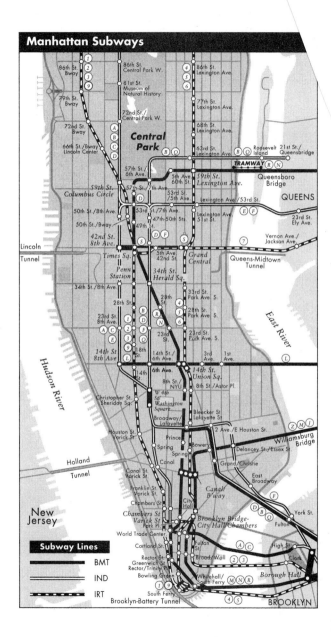

1 Essential Information

IMPORTANT CONTACTS

An Alphabetical Listing of Publications, Organizations, and Companies That Will Help You Before, During, and After Your Trip

No single travel resource can give you every detail about every topic that might interest or concern you at the various stages of your journey—when you're planning your trip, while you're on the road, and after you get back home. The following organizations, books, and brochures will supplement the information in *Fodor's Pocket New York City*. For related information, including both basic tips on visiting New York City and background information on many of the topics below, study Smart Travel Tips, the section that follows Important Contacts.

AIR TRAVEL

The major gateways to New York City are **La Guardia Airport** (☎ 718/533–3400) and **JFK International Airport** (☎ 718/244–4444), both in the borough of Queens, and **Newark International Airport** (☎ 201/961–6000) in New Jersey. Flying time is two hours from Chicago, five hours from Los Angeles.

CARRIERS

Carriers serving New York City include **America West** (☎ 800/235–9292); **American** (☎ 800/433–7300); **Continental** (☎ 800/525–0280); **Delta** (☎ 800/221–1212); **Northwest** (☎ 800/225–2525); **TWA** (☎ 800/221–2000); **United** (☎ 800/241–6522); and **USAir** (☎ 800/428–4322). For inexpensive, no-frills flights, contact **Carnival Air Lines** (☎ 800/824–7386), **Kiwi International** (☎ 800/538–5494), or **Midwest Express** (☎ 800/452–2022).

AIRPORT TRANSFERS

BY BUS

Bus companies serving one or all of the area airports include **Carey Airport Express** (☎ 718/632–0500, 800/456–1012, or 800/284–0909); **Gray Line Air Shuttle Minibus** (☎ 212/315–3006 or 800/622–3427); **Metropolitan Transit Authority** (MTA, ☎ 718/330–1234); **New Jersey Transit Airlink** and **Airport Express** (☎ 201/762–5100), and **Olympia Airport Express** (☎ 212/964–6233).

BY CAR SERVICE

Try **All State Car and Limo** (☎ 212/741–7440), **Carey Limousines** (☎ 212/599–1122), **Carmel Car and Limousine Service** (☎ 212/662–2222), **Eastside Limo Service** (☎ 212/744–9700),

Greenwich Limousine (☎ 800/385–1033), **London Towncars** (☎ 212/988–9700), **Manhattan Limo** (☎ 718/729–4200), **Sherwood Silver Bay Limousine Service** (☎ 718/472–0183), **Skyline** (☎ 212/741–3711), and **Wheels of New York** (☎ 212/255–5908).

BY HELICOPTER
For helicopter service, contact **New York Helicopter** (☎ 800/645–3494).

BY SUBWAY
For information on subway service from JFK, contact the **MTA** (☎ 718/330–1234). From Newark, you can take a **PATH Train** (☎ 800/234–7284).

BUS TRAVEL
Long-haul and commuter bus lines feed into the **Port Authority Terminal** (☎ 212/564–8484). Individual bus lines serving New York include **Greyhound Lines** (☎ 800/231–2222); **Adirondack Pine Hill Trailways** from upstate New York (☎ 800/225–6815); **Bonanza Bus Lines** (☎ 800/556–3815), **Vermont Transit** (☎ 802/862–9671), and **Peter Pan Bus Lines** (☎ 800/343–9999 or 413/781–2900) from New England; **Martz Trailways** from northeastern Pennsylvania (☎ 800/233–8604); and **New Jersey Transit** from around New Jersey (☎ 201/762–5100).

WITHIN NEW YORK CITY
For information about routes, bus stops, and hours of operation, call the **MTA** (☎ 718/330–1234) daily 6–9.

CAR RENTAL
Major car-rental companies represented in New York include **Avis** (☎ 800/331–1212, 800/879–2847 in Canada); **Budget** (☎ 800/527–0700, 0800/181–181 in the United Kingdom); **Dollar** (☎ 800/800–4000); **Hertz** (☎ 800/654–3131, 800/263–0600 in Canada, 0181/679–1799 in the United Kingdom); and **National** (☎ 800/227–7368, 0181/950–5050 in the United Kingdom, where it is known as Europcar). Rates begin at $65 a day and $205 a week for an economy car with unlimited mileage. This does not include tax, which in New York State is 13¼% on rental cars. Local companies include **Rent-A-Wreck** (☎ 212/721–0080); **Sunshine Rent-A-Car** (☎ 212/989–7260), located in Greenwich Village; and **Universal** (☎ 718/786–0786), for JFK and La Guardia arrivals.

CUSTOMS

CANADIANS
Contact **Revenue Canada** (2265 St. Laurent Blvd. S, Ottawa, Ontario, K1G 4K3, ☎ 613/993–0534) for a copy of the free brochure **"I Declare/Je Déclare"** and for details on duties that exceed the standard duty-free limit.

U.K. CITIZENS
HM Customs and Excise (Dorset House, Stamford St., London SE1

9NG, ☎ 0171/202–4227) can answer questions about U.K. customs regulations and publishes **"A Guide for Travellers,"** detailing standard procedures and import rules.

FOR TRAVELERS WITH DISABILITIES

For brochures and further information, contact the **Mayor's Office for People with Disabilities** (52 Chambers St., Office 206, New York, NY 10007, ☎ 212/788–2830, TTY 212/788–2842). In the United Kingdom, contact the **Royal Association for Disability and Rehabilitation** (RADAR, 12 City Forum, 250 City Rd., London EC1V 8AF, ☎ 0171/250–3222) or **Mobility International** (Rue de Manchester 25, B–1070 Brussels, Belgium, ☎ 00–322–410–6297), an international clearinghouse of travel information for people with disabilities.

TRAVEL AGENCIES AND TOUR OPERATORS

The Americans with Disabilities Act requires that travel firms serve the needs of all travelers. However, some agencies and operators specialize in making group and individual arrangements for travelers with disabilities, among them **Access Adventures** (206 Chestnut Ridge Rd., Rochester, NY 14624, ☎ 716/889–9096), run by a former physical-rehab counselor.

EMERGENCIES

Dial 911 for **police, fire,** or **ambulance** in an emergency (TTY is available for the hearing impaired).

The New York Telephone Company lists other important emergency and community services numbers in the front of its white-pages directory. Here are some numbers that may come in handy:

DOCTORS

Doctors On Call (☎ 212/737–2333) is a 24-hour house-call service. Near midtown, 24-hour emergency rooms are open at **St. Luke's-Roosevelt Hospital** (58th St. at 9th Ave., ☎ 212/523–6800) and **St. Vincent's Hospital** (7th Ave. and 11th St., ☎ 212/604–7997).

DENTISTS

The **Dental Emergency Service** (☎ 212/679–3966 or 212/679–4172 after 8 PM) will make referrals.

24-HOUR PHARMACIES

Kaufman's Pharmacy (Lexington Ave. and 50th St., ☎ 212/755–2266) is convenient, but its prices are exorbitant; **Genovese** (2nd Ave. at 68th St., ☎ 212/772–0104) is less expensive. Before 10 or 11 PM, look for a pharmacy in a neighborhood that keeps late hours, such as Greenwich Village or the Upper West Side, for better deals.

ENTERTAINMENT

Call the **Moviephone** (☎ 212/777–3456) to find out what movies are playing around town, including exact times and locations. Call **NYC On Stage** (☎ 212/768–1818) for up-to-the-minute information on tickets for theater, music, and dance performances.

GAY AND LESBIAN TRAVEL

The **International Gay Travel Association** (Box 4974, Key West, FL 33041, ☎ 800/448–8550), a consortium of 800 businesses, can supply names of travel agents and tour operators.

INSURANCE

Travel insurance covering baggage, health, and trip cancellation or interruptions is available from **Access America** (Box 90315, Richmond, VA 23286, ☎ 804/285–3300 or 800/284–8300); **Carefree Travel Insurance** (Box 9366, 100 Garden City Plaza, Garden City, NY 11530, ☎ 516/294–0220 or 800/323–3149); **Tele-Trip** (Mutual of Omaha Plaza, Box 31716, Omaha, NE 68131, ☎ 800/228–9792); and **Travel Insured International** (Box 280568, East Hartford, CT 06128-0568, ☎ 203/528–7663 or 800/243–3174).

IN THE U.K.

The **Association of British Insurers** (51 Gresham St., London EC2V 7HQ, ☎ 0171/600–3333; 30 Gordon St., Glasgow G1 3PU, ☎ 0141/226–3905; Scottish Provident Bldg., Donegall Sq. W, Belfast BT1 6JE, ☎ 01232/249176; call for other locations) gives advice by phone.

MONEY MATTERS

ATMS

For specific **Cirrus** locations in the United States and Canada, call 800/424–7787. For U.S. **Plus** locations, call 800/843–7587 and enter the area code and first three digits of the number you're calling from (or of the calling area where you want an ATM).

CURRENCY EXCHANGE

American Express Travel Service has nine Manhattan locations including: 822 Lexington Avenue, ☎ 212/758–6510; Bloomingdale's, 59th Street and Lexington Avenue, ☎ 212/705–3171; 150 East 42nd Street, ☎ 212/687–3700; and 374 Park Avenue, ☎ 212/421–8240.

PASSPORTS AND VISAS

U.K. CITIZENS

For fees, documentation requirements, and to get an emergency passport, call the **London Passport Office** (☎ 0171/271–3000). For visa information, call the **U.S. Embassy Visa Information Line** (☎ 0891/200290; calls cost 48p per minute or 36p per minute cheap rate) or write the **U.S. Embassy Visa Branch** (5 Upper Grosvenor St., London W1A 2JB). If you live in Northern Ireland, write the **U.S. Consulate General**

(Queen's House, Queen St., Belfast BT1 6EQ). In Scotland, apply to the consulate at 3 Regent Terrace, Edinburgh EH7 5BW.

RAIL TRAVEL

For schedules and information on national and regional rail service to New York City, contact **Amtrak** (☎ 800/872–7245), the **Long Island Railroad** (☎ 718/217–5477), **Metro-North Commuter Railroad** (☎ 212/340–3000), **New Jersey Transit** (☎ 201/762–5100), and **PATH** (☎ 800/234–7284).

SIGHTSEEING

BOAT TOURS

The most pleasant way to get a crash orientation to Manhattan is aboard a **Circle Line Cruise** (Pier 83, west end of 42nd St., ☎ 212/ 563–3200). Once you've finished the three-hour, 35-mile circumnavigation of Manhattan, you'll have a good idea of where things are and what you want to see next. Narrations are as interesting and individualized as the guides who deliver them. The fare is $18, $9 for children under 12, and the cruises are conducted daily March–December.

For a shorter excursion, **Express Navigation's** hydroliner (Pier 11, 2 blocks south of South St. Seaport, ☎ 800/262–8743) will show you the island of Manhattan in 75 minutes. The fare is $15, $13 senior citizens, $8 children under 12, children under 5 free. Boats depart April–September weekdays and Saturday at noon and 2 PM.

World Yacht Cruises (Pier 81, W. 41st St. at Hudson River, ☎ 212/ 630–8100) serves lunch ($27.50) and Sunday brunch ($39.95) on two-hour cruises, and dinner (Sun.–Fri. $62; Sat. $75; drinks extra) on three-hour cruises. The Continental cuisine is restaurant quality, and there's onboard music and dancing. The cruises run daily year-round, weather permitting.

The Spirit of New York (Pier 62, at W. 23rd St. and 12th Ave. on the Hudson River, ☎ 212/742–7278) sails on lunch ($29–$34), dinner ($53–$65), and moonlight cocktail ($20) cruises.

At South Street Seaport's Pier 16 you can take two- or three-hour voyages to New York's past aboard the iron cargo schooner *Pioneer* (☎ 212/669–9400) or one-hour sightseeing tours of New York Harbor and Lower Manhattan with **Seaport Liberty Cruises** (☎ 212/630–8888).

BUS TOURS

Gray Line (1740 Broadway, ☎ 212/397–2620) offers a taste of yesteryear with their "NY Trolley Tour" on coaches replicating New York trolleys of the '30s. The company also offers a number of standard city bus tours as well as cruises and day trips to Atlantic City. Gray Line's "Central Park Trolley Tour" tempts visitors to explore parts of the park that even native New Yorkers may have never seen.

New York Doubledecker Tours (Empire State Building at 34th St. and 5th Ave., ☎ 212/967–6008) runs authentic London double-deck buses year-round, 9–6 in summer, 10–3 in winter, making stops every 15–30 minutes at the Empire State Building, Greenwich Village, SoHo, Chinatown, the World Trade Center, Battery Park, the South Street Seaport, the United Nations, and Central Park. Tickets are valid for boarding and reboarding all day for two days; they cost $15 for adults, $10 for children under 12 and senior citizens, and may be purchased at the Empire State Building. An uptown loop, which costs $25 for adults and $15 for children and senior citizens, makes stops at Lincoln Center, the Museum of Natural History, Harlem, Museum Mile, and Central Park. Hop on and off to visit attractions as often as you like.

New York Visions (Broadway and W. 53rd St., ☎ 212/956–0517) has tours ranging from two to nine hours, including "New York Lights at Night," featuring dinner in Chinatown, a glittering skyline, jazz clubs, and nightspots.

HELICOPTER TOURS
Island Helicopter (heliport at E. 34th St. and East River, ☎ 212/683–4575) offers four flyover

options that cost from $47 (for 7 miles) to $119 (for 34 miles). From the West Side, **Liberty Helicopter Tours** (heliport at W. 30th St. and Hudson River, ☎ 212/465–8905) has four tours that cost from $45 to $129.

SPECIAL-INTEREST TOURS
Backstage on Broadway (☎ 212/575–8065) is a talk about the Broadway theater held in an actual theater, given by a theater professional. Reservations are mandatory; groups of 25 or more only. **Radio City Music Hall Productions** (☎ 212/632–4041) schedules behind-the-scenes tours of the theater. Call the **Metropolitan Opera House Backstage** (☎ 212/769–7020) for a tour of the scene and costume shops, stage area, and rehearsal facilities. **Madison Square Garden** (☎ 212/465–6080) also has tours of the sports mecca's inner workings. If TV is your thing, call **NBC Studio Tour** (☎ 212/664–7174) for a guided tour of the television studios. Architecture tours of **Grand Central Terminal** (☎ 212/986–9217) take you high above the crowds and into the Beaux Arts building's rafters. **Gracie Mansion Conservancy Tour** (☎ 212/570–4751) will show you the 1799 house, official residence of New York City mayors since 1942. **Harlem Spirituals, Inc.** (☎ 212/757–0425) and **Penny Sightseeing Co., Inc.** (☎ 212/410–0080) offer bus and walking tours and Sunday gospel

trips to Harlem. The **Lower East Side Tenement Museum** (☎ 212/431–0233) offers tours through former immigrant communities. **River to River Downtown Tours** (☎ 212/321–2823) specializes in lower Manhattan for two-hour walking tours. **Louis Singer** (☎ 718/875–9084), an encyclopedia of New York trivia, provides tours of Brooklyn and Manhattan.

SELF-GUIDED WALKING TOURS

The **New York Convention and Visitors Bureau's** "I Love New York Visitors Guide and Map" is available at the bureau's information center (2 Columbus Circle, ☎ 212/397–8222). Another option is to pop one of the **Talk-a-Walk** cassettes (Sound Publishers, 30 Waterside Plaza, New York, NY 10010-26301, ☎ 212/686–0356; $9.95 per tape, plus $2.90 packing and shipping for up to four tapes) into your Walkman and start strolling to an in-your-ear history of Lower Manhattan or the Brooklyn Bridge.

WALKING TOURS

New York City Cultural Walking Tours (☎ 212/979–2388) focuses on the city's architecture, landmarks, memorials, outdoor art, and historic sites, including Fifth Avenue's "Millionaires' Mile." **Sidewalks of New York** (☎ 212/517–0201 or 212/662–5300) hits the streets from various thematic angles—"Ye Old Tavern" tours, "Celebrity Home" tours, "Famous Murder Sites," "Chelsea Saints and Sinners," and so forth. These walks are offered on weekends year-round; weekday tours are available by appointment. **Adventure on a Shoestring** (☎ 212/265–2663) is an organization dating from 1963 that explores New York neighborhoods. Tours are scheduled periodically for $5 per person. **Big Onion Walking Tours** (☎ 212/439–1090) has theme tours: try "From Naples to Bialystok to Beijing: A Multi-Ethnic Eating Tour." The **Municipal Art Society** (☎ 212/935–3960) conducts a series of bus and walking tours.

TOUR OPERATORS

GROUP TOURS

For a deluxe escorted motor-coach tour, contact **Maupintour** (Box 807, Lawrence KS 66044, ☎ 913/843–1211 or 800/255–4266). Another operator falling between deluxe and first-class is **Globus** (5301 S. Federal Circle, Littleton, CO 80123, ☎ 303/797–2800 or 800/221–0090). In the first-class and tourist range, try **Mayflower Tours** (1225 Warren Ave., Downers Grove, IL 60515, ☎ 708/960–3430 or 800/323–7064). For budget and tourist class programs, contact **Cosmos** (*see* Globus, *above*).

PACKAGES

FROM THE U.K.➢ Tour operators offering packages to New York City include **Americana Vacations**

Ltd. (Morley House, 320 Regent St., London W1R 5AD, ☎ 0171/637–7853); **Jetsave** (Sussex House, London Rd., East Grinstead, Sussex RH19 1LD, ☎ 01342/312033); **Key to America** (1–3 Station Rd., Ashford, Middx., TW15 2UW, ☎ 01784/248777); **Premier Holidays** (Westbrook, Milton Rd., Cambridge CB4 1YQ, ☎ 01223/516688); **Trailfinders** (42–50 Earls Court Rd., London W8 6FT, ☎ 0171/937–5400; 58 Deansgate, Manchester M3 2FF, ☎ 0161/839–69693636); and **Transamerica Holidays** (3a Gatwick Metro Centre, Balcombe Rd., Horley RH6 9GA, ☎ 0293/774441).

VISITOR INFORMATION

The **New York Convention and Visitors Bureau** (2 Columbus Circle, New York, NY 10019, ☎ 212/397–8222 or 212/484–1200, FAX 212/484–1280) provides brochures, subway and bus maps, an up-to-date calendar of events, listings of hotels and weekend hotel packages, and discount coupons for Broadway shows. The office is open weekdays 9–6, weekends and holidays 10–3. The **New York State Division of Tourism** (1 Commerce Plaza, Albany, NY 12245, ☎ 518/474–4116 or 800/225–5697) offers a free series of "I Love New York" booklets listing New York City attractions and tour packages.

IN THE U.K.

Contact the **United States Travel and Tourism Administration** (Box 1EN, London W1A 1EN, ☎ 0171/495–4466). For a free USA pack, write the USTTA at Box 170, Ashford, Kent TN24 0ZX. Enclose stamps to the value of £1.50.

WEATHER

For current weather and forecasts, plus the local time and helpful travel tips, call the **Weather Channel Connection** (☎ 900/932–8437; 95¢ per minute) from a Touch-Tone phone.

SMART TRAVEL TIPS

Basic Information on Traveling in New York City and Savvy Tips to Make Your Trip a Breeze

The more you travel, the more you know about how to make trips run like clockwork. To help make your travels hassle-free, Fodor's editors have rounded up dozens of tips from our contributors and travel experts all over the world, as well as basic information on visiting New York City. For names of organizations to contact and publications that can give you more information, *see* Important Contacts, *above*.

AIR TRAVEL

If time is an issue, **always look for nonstop flights,** which require no change of plane. If possible, **avoid connecting flights,** which stop at least once and can involve a change of plane, although the flight number remains the same; if the first leg is late, the second waits.

AIRPORT TRANSFERS

LA GUARDIA AIRPORT➤ Taxis cost $14–$24 plus tolls (which may be as high as $4) and take 20–40 minutes. Group taxi rides to Manhattan are available at taxi dispatch lines just outside the baggage-claim areas during most travel hours (except on Saturday and holidays). Group fares run $8–$9 per person (plus a share of tolls).

Carey Airport Express buses depart for Manhattan every 20 minutes, 6 AM–midnight, from all terminals. It's a 40-minute ride to 42nd Street and Park Avenue, directly opposite Grand Central Terminal. The bus continues from there to the Port Authority Bus Terminal, the New York Hilton, Sheraton Manhattan, Holiday Inn Crowne Plaza, and Marriott Marquis hotels. Other midtown hotels are a short cab ride away. The bus fare is $9; pay the driver. The Gray Line Air Shuttle Minibus serves major Manhattan hotels directly to and from the airport. The fare is $13 per person; make arrangements at the airport's ground transportation center or use the courtesy phone.

JFK INTERNATIONAL AIRPORT➤ Taxis cost $25–$32 plus tolls (which may be as much as $4) and take 35–60 minutes.

Carey Airport Express buses depart for Manhattan every 30 minutes from 6 AM to midnight, from all JFK terminals. The ride to 42nd Street and Park Avenue (Grand Central Terminal) takes about one hour. The bus continues from there to the Port Authority Bus Terminal, the New York

Hilton, Sheraton Manhattan, Holiday Inn Crowne Plaza, and Marriott Marquis hotels; it's a short cab ride to other midtown hotels. The bus fare is $13; pay the driver.

The Gray Line Air Shuttle Minibus serves major Manhattan hotels directly from the airport; the cost is $16 per person. Make arrangements at the airport's ground transportation counter or use the courtesy phone.

NEWARK AIRPORT➤ Taxis cost $28–$30 plus tolls ($10) and take 20–45 minutes. "Share and Save" group rates are available for as many as four passengers between 8 AM and midnight; make arrangements with the airport's taxi dispatcher.

NJ Transit Airport Express buses (☎ 212/564–8484 or 201/762–5100) depart for the Port Authority Bus Terminal, at 8th Avenue and 42nd Street every 15 minutes from 6 AM to midnight and every hour thereafter. From there, it's a short cab ride to midtown hotels. The ride takes 30–45 minutes. The fare is $7; buy your ticket inside the airport terminal. Olympia Airport Express buses leave for Grand Central Terminal, Penn Station, and 1 World Trade Center (next to the Vista Hotel) about every 30 minutes from around 6 AM to midnight. The trip takes 35–45 minutes to Grand Central and Penn Station, 20 minutes to WTC. The fare is $7.

The Gray Line Air Shuttle Minibus serves major Manhattan hotels directly to and from the airport. You pay $18 per passenger; make arrangements at the airport's ground transportation center or use the courtesy phone.

If you are arriving in Newark, you can take New Jersey Transit's Airlink buses, which leave every 20 minutes from 6:15 AM to 2 AM, to Penn Station in Newark. The ride takes about 20 minutes; the fare is $4. From there, your can catch PATH Trains, which run to Manhattan 24 hours a day. The trains run every 10 minutes on weekdays, every 15–30 minutes on weeknights, every 20–30 minutes on weekends, and stop at the World Trade Center and at five stops along 6th Avenue—Christopher Street, 9th Street, 14th Street, 23rd Street, and 33rd Street. The fare is $1.

CAR SERVICES

Car services are a great deal, because the driver will often meet you on the concourse or in the baggage-claim area and help you with your luggage. You ride in late-model American-made cars that are comfortable, if usually a bit worn. New York City Taxi and Limousine Commission rules require that all be licensed and pick up riders only by prior arrangement. Call 24 hours in advance for reservations, or at least a half-day before your flight's departure.

BUS TRAVEL

Most buses follow easy-to-understand routes along the Manhattan grid. Routes go up or down the north–south avenues, or east and west on the major two-way crosstown streets. Most bus routes operate 24 hours, but service is infrequent late at night. Buses are great for sightseeing, but traffic jams—a potential threat at any time or place in Manhattan—can make rides maddeningly slow.

Bus fare is the same as subway fare: $1.25 at press time, in coins (no change is given) or a subway token or MetroCard (some buses will start accepting the card in 1995, and all will accept them by the end of 1996, according to the MTA). When you get on the bus, you can ask the driver for a free transfer coupon, good for one change to an intersecting route. Legal transfer points are listed on the back of the slip. Transfers have time limits of at least two hours, often longer. You cannot use the transfer to enter the subway system. Route maps and schedules are posted at many bus stops in Manhattan and at major stops throughout the other boroughs. The best places to obtain them are the Convention and Visitors Bureau at Columbus Circle or the information kiosks in Grand Central Terminal and Penn Station.

CUSTOMS AND DUTIES

IN NEW YORK

Visitors from outside the United States age 21 or over may import the following: 200 cigarettes or 50 cigars or 2 kilograms of tobacco; 1 U.S. liter of alcohol; gifts to the value of $100. Restricted items include meat products, seeds, plants, and fruits. Never carry illegal drugs.

IN THE U.K.

From countries outside the European Union, including the United States, you may import duty-free 200 cigarettes, 100 cigarillos, 50 cigars or 250 grams of tobacco; 1 liter of spirits or 2 liters of fortified or sparkling wine; 2 liters of still table wine; 60 milliliters of perfume; 250 milliliters of toilet water; plus £136 worth of other goods, including gifts and souvenirs.

FOR TRAVELERS WITH DISABILITIES

Many buildings in New York City are now wheelchair-accessible. The subway is still hard to navigate, however; people in wheelchairs do better on public buses, most of which "kneel" to facilitate getting on and off.

DRIVING

If you plan to drive into Manhattan, try to time your arrival in late morning or early afternoon. That way you'll avoid the morning and evening rush hours (a problem at the crossings into Manhattan) and lunch hour. The **Lincoln Tunnel** (I–495), **Holland Tunnel,** and **George Washington Bridge** (I–95) connect Manhattan with the New Jersey Turnpike system and points west. The Lincoln Tunnel comes into midtown Manhattan; the Holland Tunnel into lower Manhattan; and the George Washington Bridge into northern Manhattan. Each of the three arteries requires a toll ($4 for cars) eastbound into New York, but no toll westbound.

INSURANCE

BAGGAGE
Airline liability for your baggage is limited by the terms of your ticket. Insurance for losses exceeding the terms of your airline ticket can be bought directly from the airline at check-in for about $10 per $1,000 of coverage; note that it excludes a rather extensive list of items, shown on your airline ticket.

FOR U.K. TRAVELERS
According to the Association of British Insurers, a trade association representing 450 insurance companies, it's wise to **buy extra medical coverage when you visit the United States.** You can buy an annual travel-insurance policy valid for most vacations during the year in which it's purchased. If you go this route, make sure it covers you if you have a preexisting medical condition or are pregnant.

TRIP
Without insurance, you will lose all or most of your money if you must cancel your trip due to illness or any other reason. Especially if your airline ticket, cruise, or package tour is nonrefundable and cannot be changed, it's essential that you **buy trip-cancellation-and-interruption insurance.** When considering how much coverage you need, look for a policy that will cover the cost of your trip plus the nondiscounted price of a one-way airline ticket should you need to return home early.

MONEY AND EXPENSES

ATMS
Chances are that you can **use your bank card at ATMs** to withdraw money from an account and get cash advances on a credit-card account if your card has been programmed with a personal identification number, or PIN. Before leaving home, **check in on frequency limits** for withdrawals and cash advances.

TRAVELER'S CHECKS
Whether or not to buy traveler's checks depends on where you are headed; **take cash to rural areas and small towns, traveler's checks to cities.** The most widely recognized are American Express, Citicorp, Thomas Cook, and Visa, which are sold by major commercial banks for 1%–3% of the checks' face value—it pays to **shop around.**

PACKING FOR NEW YORK CITY

Jackets and ties are required for men in a number of restaurants. For sightseeing and casual dining, jeans and sneakers are acceptable just about anywhere in the city. Sneakers or other flat-heeled walking shoes are highly recommended for pounding the New York pavements; you may even see businesspeople in button-down office attire lacing them on for the sprint from one appointment to another.

Bring an extra pair of eyeglasses or contact lenses in your carry-on luggage, and if you have a health problem, **pack enough medication** to last the trip. **Don't put prescription drugs or valuables in luggage to be checked,** for it could go astray.

LUGGAGE

Free airline baggage allowances depend on the airline, the route, and the class of your ticket; ask in advance. In general, on domestic flights you are entitled to check two bags—neither exceeding 62 inches, or 158 centimeters (length + width + height), or weighing more than 70 pounds (32 kilograms). A third piece may be brought aboard; its total dimensions are generally limited to less than 45 inches (114 centimeters), so it will fit easily under the seat in front of you or in the overhead compartment. In the United States, the Federal Aviation Administration (FAA) gives airlines broad latitude to limit carry-on allowances and tailor them to different aircraft and operational conditions. Charges for excess, oversize, or overweight pieces vary.

SAFEGUARDING YOUR LUGGAGE

Before leaving home, **itemize your bags' contents** and their worth, and label them with your name, address, and phone number. (If you use your home address, cover it so that potential thieves can't see it.) Inside your bag, **pack a copy of your itinerary.** At check-in, **make sure that your bag is correctly tagged** with the airport's three-letter destination code. If your bags arrive damaged or not at all, file a written report with the airline before leaving the airport.

PASSPORTS AND VISAS

CANADIANS

No passport is necessary to enter the United States.

U.K. CITIZENS

British citizens need a valid passport. If you are staying fewer than 90 days and traveling on a vacation, with a return or onward ticket, you will probably not need a visa. However, you will need to fill out the Visa Waiver Form, 1-94W, supplied by the airline.

PERSONAL SECURITY AND COMFORT

Despite New York's bad reputation in the area of crime, most people live here for years without being robbed or assaulted. Nevertheless, as in any large city, travelers make particularly easy marks for pickpockets and hustlers, so caution is advised.

Ignore the panhandlers on the streets (some aggressive, many homeless); people who offer to hail you a cab (they often appear at Penn Station, Port Authority, and Grand Central Terminal); and limousine and gypsy cab drivers who offer you a ride. Someone who appears to have had an accident at the exit door of a bus may flee with your wallet or purse if you attempt to give aid; the individual who approaches you with a complicated story is probably playing a confidence game and hopes to get something from you. Beware of strangers jostling you in crowds, or someone tapping your shoulder from behind. Never play or place a bet on a sidewalk card game, shell game, or guessing game—they are all rigged to get your cash.

Although the subway runs round the clock, it is usually safest during the day and evening. Most residents of the city have a rough cutoff time—9 or 10 PM—past which they avoid riding the subway trains. The subway system is much safer than it once was, but to err on the side of caution, you may want to travel by bus or taxi after the theater or a concert.

RENTING A CAR

CUTTING COSTS

To get the best deal, **book through a travel agent and shop around.** When pricing cars, **ask where the rental lot is located.** Some off-airport locations offer lower rates—even though their lots are only minutes away from the terminal via complimentary shuttle. You may also want to **price local car-rental companies,** whose rates may be lower still, although service and maintenance standards may not be up to those of a national firm. Also **ask your travel agent about a company's customer-service record.** How has it responded to late plane arrivals and vehicle mishaps? Are there often lines at the rental counter, and, if you're traveling during a holiday period, does a confirmed reservation guarantee you a car?

INSURANCE

When you drive a rented car, you are generally responsible for any damage or personal injury that you cause as well as damage to the vehicle. Before you rent, **see what coverage you already have** under the terms of your personal auto-insurance policy and credit cards. For about $14 a day, rental companies sell insurance, known as a collision damage waiver (CDW), that eliminates your liability for damage to the car; it's always optional and should never be automatically added to your bill. California, New York, and Illinois have outlawed the sale of CDW altogether.

FOR U.K. CITIZENS

In the United States you must be 21 to rent a car; rates may be higher for those under 25. Extra costs cover child seats, compulsory for children under 5 (about $3 per day), and additional drivers (about $1.50 per day). To pick up your reserved car you will need the reservation voucher, a passport, a U.K. driver's license, and a travel policy covering each driver.

REST ROOMS

Public rest rooms in New York run the gamut when it comes to cleanliness. Facilities in Penn Station, Grand Central Terminal, and the Port Authority bus terminal are often quite dirty and are inhabited by homeless people. Rest rooms in subway stations have largely been sealed off because of vandalism and safety concerns.

As a rule, the cleanest bathrooms are in midtown department stores such as Macy's, Lord & Taylor, and Bloomingdale's, in museums, or in the lobbies of large hotels. Public atriums, such as the Citicorp Center and Trump Tower, also provide good public facilities, as does the newly renovated Bryant Park. A program to install self-cleaning pay toilets (25¢) in other parks is now underway. Restaurants, too, have rest rooms, but usually just for patrons. If you're dressed well and look as if you belong, you can often just sail right on in. Be aware that cinemas, Broadway theaters, and concert halls have limited amenities, and there are often long lines before performances and during intermissions.

SUBWAYS

The 714-mile subway system operates 24 hours a day and, especially within Manhattan, serves most of the places you'll want to visit. It's cheaper than a cab and, during the workweek, often faster than either cabs or buses. The trains have been rid of their graffiti (some New Yorkers, of course, miss the colorful old trains), and sleek, new, air-conditioned cars predominate on every line. Still, the New York subway is not problem-free. Many trains are crowded and noisy. Although trains usually run frequently, especially during rush hours, you never know when some incident somewhere on the line will stall traffic. Unsavory characters lurk around certain stations, and panhandlers frequently work their way through the cars. Don't write off the subway—some 3.5 million passengers ride it every day without incident—but stay alert at all times (see Personal Security and Comfort, above).

The subway fare at press time was $1.25, but transit authority officials were already predicting that it would be raised to $1.50, which may have occurred by the time you visit New York. Reduced fares are available for people with disabilities and senior citizens during nonrush hours. If you're just taking a few trips, you should pay with tokens; they are sold at token booths that are *usually* open at each station, as well as token vending machines. It is advisable to buy several tokens at one time to prevent waiting in line later.

Most subway entrances are at street corners and are marked by lampposts with globe-shape green lights. Subway lines are named with numbers and letters, such as the No. 3 or the A. Some lines run "express" and skip lots of stops; others are "locals" and make all stops. Each station entrance has a sign indicating the lines that run through the station; some stations are also marked "uptown only" or "downtown only." Before entering subway stations, read the signs carefully–one of the most frequent mistakes visitors make is taking the train in the wrong direction—although this can be an adventure, it can also be frustrating if you're in a hurry. This book's subway map covers the most-visited parts of Manhattan. Maps of the full subway system are posted on trains and at stations. You can usually pick up free maps at token booths, too.

For route information, ask the token clerk or a transit policeman.

Call 718/330–1234 (a local call, 25¢ from pay phones) for information from 6 AM to 9 PM daily. And don't hesitate to ask a fellow rider for directions: Once New Yorkers realize you're harmless, most bend over backward to be helpful.

TAXIS

Taxis are usually easy to hail on the street or from a taxi rank in front of major hotels. You can tell if a cab is available by checking its rooftop light; if the center panel is lit, the driver is ready to take passengers. Taxis cost $1.50 for the first ⅕ mile, 25¢ for each ⅕ mile thereafter, and 25¢ for each 75 seconds not in motion. A 50¢ surcharge is added to rides begun between 8 PM and 6 AM. There is no charge for extra passengers, but you must pay any bridge or tunnel tolls incurred during your trip (sometimes a driver will personally pay a toll to keep moving quickly, but that amount will be added to the fare when the ride is over). Taxi drivers also expect a 15% tip. Barring performance above and beyond the call of duty, don't feel obliged to give them more.

To avoid unhappy taxi experiences, try to have a general idea of where you want to go. A few cab drivers are dishonest; some are ignorant; some can barely understand English. If you have no idea of the proper route, you may be taken for a long and costly ride.

TELEPHONES

There are more than 58,000 public telephones in New York City, nearly 25,000 of which are in Manhattan. A visitor should never have to hunt more than three or four blocks before finding a coin-operated phone.

The area code for Manhattan is 212; for Brooklyn, Queens, the Bronx, and Staten Island, it's 718. Dial 1 and the area code when calling from Manhattan to the outer boroughs or vice versa. Pay telephones cost 25¢ for the first three minutes of a local call (this includes calls between 212 and 718 area codes); an extra deposit is required for each additional minute.

TIPPING

The customary tipping rate is 15%–20% for taxi drivers and waiters; bellhops are usually given $2 in luxury hotels, $1 elsewhere. Hotel maids should be tipped around $1 per day of your stay.

WHEN TO GO

At one time, it seemed New York's cultural life was limited to the months between October and May, when new Broadway shows opened, museums mounted major exhibitions, and formal seasons for opera, ballet, and concerts held sway. Today, however, there are Broadway openings even in mid-July, and a number of touring orchestras and opera and ballet companies visit the city in summer. In late spring and summer, the streets and parks are filled with ethnic parades, impromptu sidewalk concerts, and free performances under the stars. Except for regular closing days and a few holidays (such as Christmas, New Year's Day, and Thanksgiving), the city's museums are open year-round. The parks are always free, so in winter you can cross-country ski, in summer you can swim or sunbathe, and in summer and fall you can watch migrating birds make their semiannual New York visits.

CLIMATE

Although there's an occasional bone-chilling winter day, with winds blasting in off the Hudson, snow only occasionally accumulates in the city. Summer is the only unpleasant time of year, especially the humid, hot days of August, when many Manhattanites vacate the island for summer homes. Most hotels are air-conditioned, but if you're traveling in the summer and choosing budget accommodations, it's a good idea to ask whether your room has an air conditioner. Air-conditioned stores, restaurants, theaters, and museums provide respite from the heat; so do the many green expanses of parks. Subways and buses are usually air-conditioned, but subway stations can be as hot as saunas.

2 Exploring Manhattan

MANHATTAN IS, ABOVE ALL, A walker's city. Along its busy streets there's something else to look at every few yards. The city's character changes every few blocks, from quaint town houses shouldering sleek glass towers to gleaming gourmet supermarkets sitting around the corner from dusty thrift shops. Many a visitor has been beguiled into walking a little farther, then a little farther still, and ending up with a severe case of blisters. So be warned: Wear your most comfortable shoes, preferably sneakers, and take time along the way to stop and rest.

Orientation

Above 14th Street, the streets form a regular grid pattern, imposed in 1811. Consecutively numbered streets run east and west (crosstown), while broad avenues, most of them also numbered, run north (uptown) or south (downtown). The chief exceptions are Broadway (which runs on a diagonal from East 14th to West 79th streets) and the thoroughfares that hug the shores of the Hudson and East rivers.

Fifth Avenue is the east–west dividing line for street addresses: in both directions, they increase in regular increments from there. For example, on 55th Street, the addresses 1–99 East 55th Street run from 5th, past Madison, to Park (the equivalent of 4th) avenues, 100–199 East 55th would be between Park and 3rd avenues, and so on; the addresses 1–99 West 55th Street are between 5th and 6th avenues, 100–199 West 55th would be between 6th and 7th avenues, and so forth. Avenue addresses are much less regular—an address at 552 3rd Avenue, for example, will not necessarily be anywhere near 552 2nd Avenue. Many New Yorkers themselves cannot master the complexities of this system, so in their daily dealings they usually include cross-street references along with avenue addresses. New Yorkers also rely on the handy Manhattan Address Locator found in the front of the local phone book.

Below 14th Street—the area that was already settled before the 1811 grid was decreed—Manhattan streets are dis-

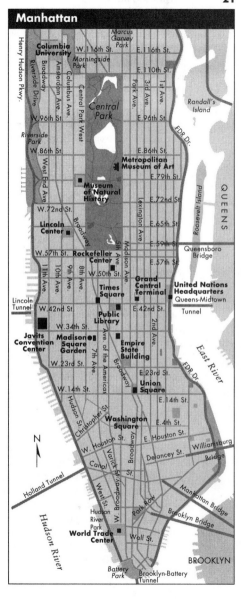

Manhattan

Henry Hudson Pkwy.

Columbia University

W.116th St.
E.116th St.

Marcus Garvey Park

Morningside Park

E.110th St.

Broadway
Amsterdam Ave.
Columbus Ave.
Central Park West

Central Park

Park Ave.
3rd Ave.
1st Ave.

Randall's Island

W.96th St.
E.96th St.

Riverside Drive
Riverside Park

FDR Dr.

W.86th St.
E.86th St.

West End Ave.

Metropolitan Museum of Art
E.79th St.

Museum of Natural History
E.72nd St.

Lexington Ave.

QUEENS

W.72nd St.
E.65th St.

Roosevelt Island

Lincoln Center
E.59th St.

Broadway

W.57th St.
Rockefeller Center
Queensboro Bridge

9th Ave.
8th Ave.
W.50th St.
E.57th St.

Madison Ave.
5th Ave.

11th Ave.
10th Ave.

Times Square
Grand Central Terminal

United Nations Headquarters

Lincoln Tunnel

W.42nd St.
E.42nd St.
Queens-Midtown Tunnel

Public Library

Javits Convention Center
W.34th St.

Madison Square Garden
Empire State Building
2nd Ave.

7th Ave.
Ave. of the Americas

W.23rd St.
E.23rd St.

Broadway
FDR Dr.

East River

W.14th St.
Union Square
E.14th St.

Hudson St.
Christopher St.
Washington Square
E.4th St.

W. Houston St.
E. Houston St.

Varick St.
Broadway
Delancey St.
Williamsburg Bridge

N

Canal St.

Holland Tunnel

West St.
Park Row

Manhattan Bridge

Hudson River
Hudson River Park
Brooklyn Bridge

World Trade Center
Wall St.

BROOKLYN

Battery Park
Brooklyn-Battery Tunnel

ordered. They may be aligned with the shoreline or they may twist along the route of an ancient cow path. There's an East Broadway and a West Broadway, both of which run north–south and neither of which is an extension of plain old Broadway. Logic won't help you below 14th Street; only a good street map and good directions will.

You may also be confused by the way New Yorkers use "uptown" and "downtown." These terms refer both to locations and to directions. Uptown means north of wherever you are at the moment; downtown means to the south. But Uptown and Downtown are also specific parts of the city (and, some would add, two very distinct states of mind). Unfortunately, there is no consensus about where these areas are: Downtown may mean anyplace from the tip of Lower Manhattan through Chelsea; it depends on the orientation of the speaker.

A similar situation exists with "East Side" and "West Side." Someone may refer to a location as "on the east side," meaning somewhere east of 5th Avenue. A hotel described as being "on the west side" may be on West 42nd Street. But when New Yorkers speak of the East Side or the West Side, they usually mean the respective areas above 59th Street, on either side of Central Park. Be prepared for misunderstandings.

Tour 1: Rockefeller Center

Numbers in the margin correspond to points of interest on the Midtown map.

Begun during the Great Depression of the 1930s by John D. Rockefeller, this 19-building complex occupies nearly 22 acres of prime real estate between 5th and 7th avenues and 47th and 52nd streets. The central buildings are smooth shafts of warm-hued limestone, streamlined with glistening aluminum, but the real genius of the complex's design was its intelligent use of public space: plazas, concourses, and street-level shops that create a sense of community for the nearly quarter of a million human beings who use it daily.

Let's begin the tour with a proud symbol of the center's might: the huge statue of Atlas supporting the world that
❶ stands sentry before the **International Building** (5th Ave., between 50th and 51st Sts.). The building, with a lobby inspired by ancient Greece and fitted with Grecian marble, houses many foreign consulates, international airlines, and a U.S. passport office.

One block south on 5th Avenue, between 49th and 50th streets, you'll come to the head of the **Channel Gardens,** a promenade with six pools surrounded by flowerbeds filled with seasonal plantings, conceived by artists, floral designers, and sculptors—10 shows a season. They are called the Channel Gardens because they separate the British building to the north from the French building to the south (above each building's entrance is a coat of arms bearing that country's national symbols).

At the foot of the Channel Gardens is perhaps the most famous sight in Rockefeller Center: the great gold-leaf statue of the fire-stealing Greek hero **Prometheus,** sprawled on his
❷ ledge above the **Lower Plaza.** A quotation from Aeschylus is carved into the red granite wall behind, and 50 jets of water spray around the statue. The plaza's trademark ice-skating rink is open from October through April; the rest of the year, it becomes an open-air café. In December the plaza is decorated with an enormous live Christmas tree. On the Esplanade above the Lower Plaza, flags of the United Nations' members alternate with flags of the states.

❸ The 70-story **GE Building** (formerly the RCA Building until GE acquired RCA in 1986), occupying the block bounded by Rockefeller Plaza, Avenue of the Americas (which New Yorkers call 6th Avenue), and 49th and 50th streets is the center's tallest tower. The block-long street called Rockefeller Plaza, officially a private street (to maintain that status, it closes to all traffic on one day a year), is often choked with celebrities' black limousines, for this is the headquarters of the NBC television network. From this building emanated some of the first TV programs ever. The *Today* show used to originate from the GE building, but it is now broadcast from a ground-floor, glass-enclosed studio on the southwest corner of 49th Street and Rockefeller

24

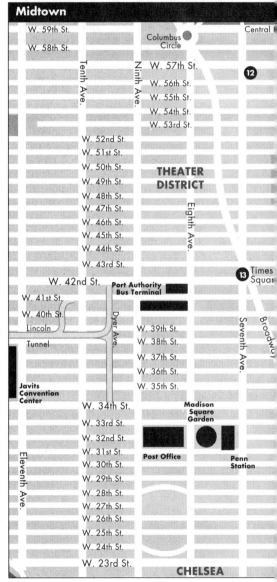

Midtown

W. 59th St.

W. 58th St.

Columbus Circle

Central

Tenth Ave.

Ninth Ave.

W. 57th St.

⑫

W. 56th St.

W. 55th St.

W. 54th St.

W. 53rd St.

W. 52nd St.

W. 51st St.

W. 50th St.

W. 49th St.

THEATER DISTRICT

W. 48th St.

W. 47th St.

W. 46th St.

Eighth Ave.

W. 45th St.

W. 44th St.

W. 43rd St.

W. 42nd St.

Port Authority Bus Terminal

⑬ Times Squar

W. 41st St.

W. 40th St.

Lincoln

Tunnel

Dyer Ave.

W. 39th St.

W. 38th St.

W. 37th St.

Seventh Ave.

Broadway

W. 36th St.

W. 35th St.

Javits Convention Center

W. 34th St.

Madison Square Garden

W. 33rd St.

W. 32nd St.

W. 31st St.

W. 30th St.

Post Office

Penn Station

Eleventh Ave.

W. 29th St.

W. 28th St.

W. 27th St.

W. 26th St.

W. 25th St.

W. 24th St.

W. 23rd St.

CHELSEA

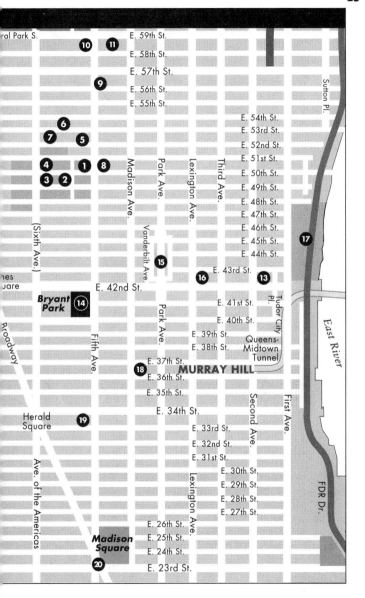

Plaza. If you're in the area between 7 and 9 AM, your face may show up on TV behind Katie and Bryant.

One way to see what goes on inside is to spend $8.25 to take a tour of the NBC studios: One leaves from the street level of the GE Building every 15 minutes, 9:30–4:30, Monday–Saturday, and on Sunday during the summer. (Children under 6 are not permitted.)

As you enter the GE Building from Rockefeller Plaza, look up at the striking sculpture of Zeus above the entrance doors, executed in limestone cast in glass by Lee Lawrie, the same artist who sculpted the big Atlas on 5th Avenue. From the lobby information desk, go down the escalator in the right-hand corner and turn right to find a detailed exhibit on the history of the center (☛ Free; open weekdays 9–5).

Returning to the GE Building lobby, you can take an elevator to the 65th floor to enjoy the spectacular view with drinks or a meal at the **Rainbow Room.**

Across 50th Street from the GE Building is America's largest **❹** indoor theater, the 6,000-seat **Radio City Music Hall.** Home of the fabled Rockettes chorus line (which actually started out in St. Louis in 1925), Radio City was built as a movie theater with a stage suitable for live shows as well. Its days as a first-run movie house are long over, but after an announced closing in 1978 Radio City has had an amazing comeback, producing concerts and special events, along with its own Christmas and Easter extravaganzas. On most days you can take a one-hour tour of the premises. ☎ 212/247–4777; tour information, 212/632–4041. Tour ☛ $10 adults, $5 children under 6. Tours usually leave from main lobby every 30 mins, daily, 10–5.

From here, you can choose among a cluster of museums: the Museum of Television and Radio, the American Craft Museum, or the world-renowned Museum of Modern Art. **❺** Go east on 52nd Street to the **Museum of Television and Radio,** housed in a new limestone building by Philip Johnson and John Burgee. Three galleries exhibit photographs and artifacts relating to the history of broadcasting, but most visitors to this museum come to sit at a console and sample its stupendous collection of more than 32,000 TV shows, 13,000 commercials, and 16,000 radio programs. *25 W. 52nd St.,* ☎ *212/621–6800 for daily events or 212/621–6600 for other information. Suggested contribution: $6 adults, $4 students and senior citizens, $3 children under 13.* ☉ *Tues.–Sun. noon–6, Thurs. noon–8.*

Just east of the Museum of Television and Radio, you'll pass the famous restaurant **The "21" Club,** with its trademark row of jockey statuettes parading along the wrought-iron balcony. Now wonderfully restored after an extensive renovation, it still has a burnished men's-club atmosphere and a great downstairs bar.

To reach the other museums, on 53rd Street, walk toward 5th Avenue and turn left to cut through the shopping arcade of 666 5th Avenue. On the north side of 53rd is the **Museum of Modern Art** (MOMA), in a bright and airy six-story structure built around a secluded sculpture garden. In the second-and third-floor galleries of painting and sculpture, some of the world's most famous modern paintings are displayed: Van Gogh's *Starry Night,* Picasso's *Les Demoiselles d'Avignon,* Matisse's *Dance.* The collection also includes photography, architecture, decorative arts, drawings, prints, illustrated books, and films. Afternoon and evening film shows, mostly foreign films and classics, are free with the price of admission. Programs change daily; call 212/708–9480 for a schedule. Free jazz concerts are given in the café on Friday evenings. Don't miss the MOMA Design Store across the street *11 W. 53rd St.,* ☎ *212/708–9480.* ☛ *$8 adults, $5 students and senior citizens. Pay what you wish Thurs. and Fri. 5:30–8:30.* ☉ *Sat.–Tues. 11–6, Thurs. and Fri. noon–8:30.*

❼ On the south side of 53rd, the **American Craft Museum** spotlights the work of contemporary American and international craftspersons working in clay, glass, fabric, wood, metal, paper, or even chocolate. Distinctions between "craft" and "high art" become irrelevant here, for much of this work is provocative and fun to look at. *40 W. 53rd St.,* ☎ *212/956–3535.* ☛ *$5 adults, $2.50 students and senior citizens.* ☉ *Tues. 10–8, Wed.–Sun. 10–5.*

For a look at some of the city's landmark skyscrapers, head east on 53rd Street across 5th Avenue. At Madison Avenue, you may want to detour left (north) to 55th Street to see the **Sony Building,** designed by architect Philip Johnson (former tenant AT&T has moved to New Jersey). Unlike the sterile ice-cube-tray buildings of 6th Avenue, Sony's rose granite columns, its regilded statue of the winged *Golden Boy* in the lobby, and its peculiar "Chippendale" roof have made it an instant landmark for New Yorkers, who consider it the first postmodern skyscraper. The first floor, Sony Plaza, includes a public seating area, a music store where you can purchase recordings, and the new **Sony Wonder Technology Lab,** outfitted with tremendously entertaining interactive exhibits such as a recording studio, a video-game production studio, and a TV production studio. ☎ *212/833–8830.* ☛ *Free.* ☉ *Tues.–Sat. 10–6, Sun. noon–6.*

Tour 2: 5th Avenue and 57th Street

Numbers in the margin correspond to points of interest on the Midtown map.

The stretch of 5th Avenue upward from Rockefeller Center glitters with elegant shops, but the rents are even higher along East 57th Street, a parade of very exclusive smaller shops and upmarket art galleries. This is one of the world's great shopping districts, and every year more and more international fashion firms try to muscle in on this turf. The list of designer boutiques reads like a roll call of haute couture—Dior, Gucci, Vuitton, Ferragamo, Fendi, Chanel. If your goal here is to spend a lot of money, *see* Chapter 3 for more details.

❽ Across 50th Street from Rockefeller Center is the Gothic-style **St. Patrick's,** the Roman Catholic cathedral of New York. Dedicated to the patron saint of the Irish—then and now one of New York's principal ethnic groups—the white marble and stone structure was begun in 1858, consecrated in 1879, and completed in 1906. From outside, catch one of the city's most photographed views: the ornate white spires of St. Pat's against the black glass curtain of **Olympic Tower,** a multiuse building of shops, offices, and luxury apartments.

❾ **Trump Tower,** on 5th Avenue between 56th and 57th streets, is an exclusive 68-story apartment and office building named for its developer, Donald Trump. The 5th Avenue entrance leads into a glitzy six-story shopping atrium paneled in pinkish-orange marble and trimmed with lustrous brass. A fountain cascades against one wall, drowning out the clamor of the city.

The intersection of 5th Avenue and 57th Street is ground zero for high-class shopping. And what more fitting resident for this spot than **Tiffany & Co.** (727 5th Ave.), the renowned jeweler, with its Fort Knox–like Art Deco entrance. One quintessential New York movie, *Breakfast at Tiffany's,* opens with Audrey Hepburn, dressed in an evening gown, emerging from a yellow cab at dawn to stand here window-shopping with coffee and a Danish.

Cross 57th Street and head back toward 5th Avenue on the north side of the street, with its stellar lineup of boutiques: The newest addition to the block is the **Warner Brothers Studio Store** (1 E. 57th St.) with loads of movie and cartoon paraphernalia.

⑩ Appropriately named **The Plaza,** the famous hotel (*see* Chapter 5) at the western edge of this square is a registered historical landmark built in 1907. Its architect, Henry Hardenbergh, achieved a sprightly birthday-cake effect with white-glazed brick busily decorated and topped off with a copper-and-slate mansard roof. The hotel has been featured in many movies, from Alfred Hitchcock's *North by Northwest* to more recent films such as *Arthur* and *Home Alone 2.* Among the many upper-crust parties that have taken place in the Plaza's ballroom was Truman Capote's Black and White Ball of 1966, attended by everyone who was anyone—all dressed, naturally, in black and white.

⑪ Adjacent to Grand Army Plaza stands the **General Motors Building,** a 50-story tower of Georgia marble. One section of the main floor is the flagship of the legendary **F.A.O. Schwarz** toy store, with its fantastic mechanical clock right inside the front doors. Bigger than it looks from outside, the toy-o-rama offers a vast, wondrously fun selection, although it definitely tends toward expensive imports. Browsing here should bring out the child in everyone.

On your way to Carnegie Hall, you may want to cross the street to grab a bite (or at least steal a peek) at **Planet Hollywood** (140 W. 57th St., ☎ 212/333–7827), where, behind the pink-and-green striped awnings and plastic palm trees, you'll find a trendy restaurant stuffed with movie memorabilia—everything from Humphrey Bogart's Maltese Falcon to *Star Wars'* R2D2 and C3PO robots. A few doors down from Planet Hollywood is the more staid, but no less celebrity-studded, **Russian Tea Room** restaurant (150 W. 57th St., ☎ 212/265–0947) with its red awning and black marble and brass facing.

Presiding over the southeast corner of 7th Avenue and 57th
⑫ Street, **Carnegie Hall** has been hosting musical headliners since 1891, when its first concert was conducted by no less than Tchaikovsky. Outside it's a stout, square brown building with a few Moorish-style arches added, almost as an afterthought, to the facade. Inside, however, is a simply decorated, 2,804-seat auditorium that is considered one of the finest in the world. Guided tours of Carnegie Hall are also available (they last about 45 minutes). *Carnegie Hall Museum: 881 7th Ave., ☎ 212/903–9629. ☛ Free. ☉ Mon., Tues., Thurs.–Sun. 11–4:30. Guided tours (☎ 212/247–7800) offered Mon., Tues., Thurs., and Fri. 11:30, 2, and 3 (performance schedule permitting); ☛ $6 adults, $5 students and seniors, $3 children under 12.*

Devotees of classical music may want to head from here up to nearby Lincoln Center (*see* Tour 7, *below*).

A few blocks south and west is the old **Ed Sullivan Theater** (1697 Broadway, between 53rd and 54th Sts.), now home to the "David Letterman Show."

Tour 3: Across 42nd Street

Numbers in the margin correspond to points of interest on the Midtown map.

While it may not exactly be the Crossroads of the World,
★ ⑬ as it is often called, **Times Square** is one of New York's principal energy centers. It's one of many New York City "squares" that are actually triangles formed by the angle of Broadway slashing across a major avenue—in this case,

crossing 7th Avenue at 42nd Street. The square itself is occupied by the former Times Tower, now resheathed in
white marble and called **One Times Square Plaza.** When
the *New York Times* moved into its new headquarters on
December 31, 1904, it publicized the event with a fireworks
show at midnight, thus starting a New Year's Eve tradition.
Each December 31, workmen on this roof lower a 200-
pound ball down the flagpole by hand, just as they have
since 1908. The huge intersection below is mobbed with
revelers, and when the ball hits bottom on the stroke of midnight, pandemonium ensues.

From 44th to 51st streets, the cross streets west of Broadway are lined with some 30 major theaters (*see* Chapter 6).
This has been the city's main theater district since the turn
of the century; movie theaters joined the fray beginning in
the 1920s. As the theaters drew crowds of people in the
evenings, advertisers began to mount huge electric signs here,
which gave the intersection its distinctive nighttime glitter.

⓴ Between 40th and 42nd streets on 5th Avenue, you'll find
the central research building of the **New York Public Library.**
This 1911 masterpiece of Beaux Arts design was financed
largely by John Jacob Astor, whose previous library building downtown has since been turned into the Public Theater. Its grand front steps are guarded by two crouching
marble lions—dubbed "Patience" and "Fortitude" by
Mayor Fiorello La Guardia, who said he visited the facility to "read between the lions." After admiring the white
marble neoclassical facade (crammed with statues, as is typ-
ical of Beaux Arts buildings), walk through the bronze
front doors into the grand marble lobby with its sweeping
double staircase. Then take a (quiet) look upstairs at the
huge, high-ceilinged main reading room, a haven of schol-
arly calm, or visit the current exhibition in the art gallery.
Free one-hour tours, each as individual as the library vol-
unteer who leads it, are given Tuesday–Saturday at 11 AM
and 2 PM. ☎ 212/930–0800. ⊘ *Tues.–Wed. 11–7:30,
Thurs.–Sat. 10–6.*

⓯ Continue east on 42nd Street to **Grand Central Terminal** (not
a "station," as many people call it, since all runs begin or
end here). Constructed between 1903 and 1913, this Man-

hattan landmark was originally designed by a Minnesota architectural firm and later gussied up with Beaux Arts ornamentation. If you can handle it, the best time to visit is at rush hour, when the cavernous main concourse crackles with the frenzy of scurrying commuters, dashing every which way. *Tours given every Wed. at 12:30 PM (meet in front of Chemical Bank inside terminal on main level). Tours free, but donations to Municipal Art Society are accepted, ☎ 212/935–3960.*

16 Ask New Yorkers to name their favorite skyscraper and most will choose the Art Deco **Chrysler Building** at 42nd Street and Lexington Avenue. Although the Chrysler Corporation itself moved out a long time ago, this graceful shaft culminating in a stainless-steel spire still captivates the eye and the imagination. The building has no observation deck, but you can go inside its elegant dark lobby, which is faced with African marble and covered with a ceiling mural that salutes transportation and human endeavor.

★ **17** The **United Nations Headquarters** complex occupies a lushly landscaped 18-acre riverside tract just east of 1st Avenue between 42nd and 48th streets. A line of flagpoles with banners representing the current roster of 159 member nations stands before the striking 550-foot-high slab of the Secretariat Building, with the domed General Assembly Building nestled at its side. The headquarters were designed during 1947–53 by an international team of architects led by Wallace Harrison. You can enter the General Assembly Building at the 46th Street door; the interior corridors overflow with imaginatively diverse artwork donated by member nations. Free tickets to most sessions are available on a first-come, first-served basis 15 minutes before sessions begin; pick them up in the General Assembly lobby. (The full General Assembly is in session from the third Tuesday in September to the end of December.) *Visitor entrance: 1st Ave. and 46th St., ☎ 212/963–7713. Tours daily 9:15–4:45, in Jan. and Feb. tours weekdays only. 45-min tours in English leave the General Assembly lobby every 30 min. Tour ☛ $6.50 adults, $4.50 students and senior citizens, $3.50 students in 8th grade and under. Children under 5 not permitted.*

Tour 4: Murray Hill to Gramercy Park

Numbers in the margin correspond to points of interest on the Midtown map.

As the city grew progressively north throughout the 19th century, one neighborhood after another had its fashionable heyday, only to fade from glory. But three neighborhoods, east of 5th Avenue roughly between 20th and 40th streets, have preserved much of their historic charm, in Murray Hill's brownstone mansions and town houses, Madison Square's classic turn-of-the-century skyscrapers, and Gramercy Park's London-like leafy square. The only "must-see" along this route is the Empire State Building, but the walk as a whole is worth taking for the many moments en route when you may feel as if you've stepped back in time.

On East 36th Street, between Madison and Park avenues, the **Pierpont Morgan Library** is built around the famous banker's own study and library, completed in 1906 by McKim, Mead & White. Around the corner, at 37th Street and Madison Avenue, is the latest addition to the library, an 1852 Italianate brownstone that was once the home of Morgan's son, J. P. Morgan, Jr. The elder Morgan's own house stood at 36th Street and Madison Avenue; it was torn down after his death and replaced with the simple neoclassical annex that today holds the library's main exhibition space. You can go inside and visit the galleries for rotating exhibitions; go straight to see items from the permanent collection, principally drawings, prints, manuscripts, and rare books, and to pass through the new glass-roofed garden court to the fine bookstore. *29 E. 36th St.,* ☎ *212/685–0008. Suggested contribution: $5 adults, $3 students and senior citizens.* ☉ *Tues.–Fri. 10:30–5, Sat. 10:30–6, Sun. noon–6.*

The **Empire State Building** may no longer be the world's tallest building, but it is certainly one of the world's best-loved skyscrapers. The Art Deco playground for King Kong opened in 1931 after only about a year of construction. The crowning spire was originally designed as a mooring mast for dirigibles, but none ever docked here; in 1951, a TV transmittal tower was added to the top, raising the total height to 1,472 feet. Today more than 16,000 people work in the building, and more than 2½ million people a year visit the 86th- and 102nd-floor observatories. Go to the concourse level to buy a ticket for the observation decks. The 102nd-floor spot is glassed in; the 86th floor is open to the air. *350 5th Ave. at 34th St., ☎ 212/736-3100. ☛ $4 adults, $2 senior citizens and children 5–11. ☉ Daily 9:30 AM–midnight; last elevator up leaves at 11:30 PM.*

⓴ The Renaissance-style **Flatiron Building,** by architect Daniel Burnham, occupies the triangular lot formed by Broadway, 5th Avenue, and 23rd Street. This, too, was the tallest building in the world when it opened (1902). Its rounded front point is only 6 feet wide, but gentle waves built into the molded limestone-and-terra-cotta side walls soften the wedge effect. Originally named the Fuller Building, it was instantly rechristened by the public because of its resemblance to a flatiron, and eventually the nickname became official.

Union Square lies between Park Avenue South and Broadway and 14th and 17th streets. Its name, originally signifying the fact that two main roads merged here, proved doubly apt in the early 20th century when the square became a rallying spot for labor protests and mass demonstrations. If possible, visit on Greenmarket day (Monday, Wednesday, Friday, and Saturday), when farmers from all over the Northeast bring their goods to the big town: fresh produce, homemade bakery goods, cheeses, cider, New York State wines, even fish and meat.

Tour 5: Museum Mile

Numbers in the margin correspond to points of interest on the Museum Mile and Central Park map.

Once known as Millionaire's Row, the stretch of 5th Avenue between 79th and 104th streets has been fittingly renamed Museum Mile, for it now contains an impressive cluster of cultural institutions. The connection is more than coincidental: Many museums are housed in what used to be the great mansions of merchant princes and wealthy industrialists. In 1979 a group of 10 5th Avenue institutions formed a consortium that, among other activities, sponsors a Museum Mile Festival each June. The Frick Collection and the Whitney Museum of American Art are not officially part of the Museum Mile Consortium, but they're located close enough to be added to this tour.

It would be impossible to do justice to all these collections in one outing. You may want to select one or two museums to linger in and simply walk past the others, appreciating their exteriors (this in itself constitutes a minicourse in modern architecture). Save the rest for another day—or for your next trip to New York.

Be sure to pick the right day of the week for this tour. Most of these museums are closed on Monday, and some are free during extended hours on Tuesday or Thursday evening.

★ ❶ Begin at 5th Avenue and 70th Street with **The Frick Collection,** housed in an ornate, imposing Beaux Arts mansion built in 1914 for coke-and-steel baron Henry Clay Frick, who wanted the superb art collection he was amassing to be kept far from the soot and smoke of Pittsburgh, where he'd made his fortune. Strolling through the mansion, one can imagine how it felt to live with Vermeers by the front stairs, Gainsborough and Reynolds portraits in the dining room, canvases by Constable and Turner in the library, and Titians, Holbeins, a Giovanni Bellini, and an El Greco in the living room. *1 E. 70th St.,* ☎ *212/288–0700.* ☛ *$5 adults, $3 students and senior citizens. Children under 10 not admitted.* ☉ *Tues.–Sat. 10–6, Sun. 1–6, closed holidays.*

Walk one block east to Madison Avenue and head up to ❷ 75th Street to **The Whitney Museum of American Art.** This museum grew out of a gallery in the studio of the sculptor and collector Gertrude Vanderbilt Whitney, whose talent and taste were fortuitously accompanied by the wealth of two prominent families. The current building, opened in 1966, is a minimalist gray granite vault, separated from Madison Avenue by a dry moat; it was designed by Marcel Breuer, a member of the Bauhaus school, which prized functionality in architecture. The changing exhibitions offer an intelligent survey of 20th-century American works; the second floor offers, among other exhibits, daring new work from American video artists and filmmakers, and the third-floor gallery features a sample of the permanent col-

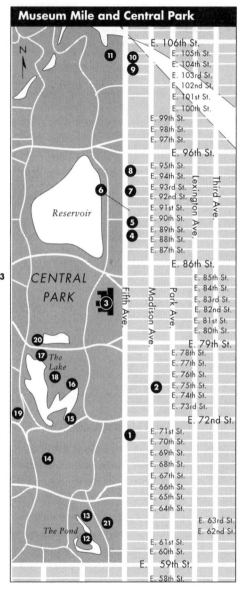

Museum Mile and Central Park

lection, including Edward Hopper's haunting *Early Sunday Morning* (1930), Georgia O'Keeffe's *White Calico Flower* (1931), and Jasper Johns's *Three Flags* (1958). *945 Madison Ave. at 75th St.,* ☏ *212/570–3676.* ☛ *$7 adults, $5 students and senior citizens.* ◎ *Wed., Fri.–Sun. 11–6, Thurs. 1–8.*

★ ❸ The **Metropolitan Museum of Art** offers valid evidence for billing itself as "New York's number one tourist attraction"; certainly the quality and range of its holdings make it one of the world's greatest museums. It's the largest art museum in the Western Hemisphere (1.6 million square feet), and its permanent collection of more than 3 million works of art from all over the world includes objects from prehistoric to modern times. The museum, founded in 1870, moved to this location in 1880, but the original redbrick building by Calvert Vaux has since been encased in other architecture. The majestic 5th Avenue facade, designed by Richard Morris Hunt, was built in 1902 of gray Indiana limestone; later additions eventually surrounded the original building on the sides and back. (On a side wall of the new ground-floor European Sculpture Court, you can glimpse the museum's original redbrick facade.)

The 5th Avenue entrance leads into the Great Hall, a soaring neoclassical chamber that has been designated a landmark. Past the entrance booths, a vast marble staircase leads up to the European painting galleries, whose highlights include Botticelli's *The Last Communion of St. Jerome* and Rembrandt's *Aristotle with a Bust of Homer.* The arcaded European Sculpture Court includes Auguste Rodin's massive bronze *The Burghers of Calais.*

American art has its own wing, back in the northwest corner; start on the first floor, where you enter through a refreshingly light and airy garden court graced with Tiffany stained-glass windows, cast-iron staircases by Louis Sullivan, and a marble Federal-style facade taken from the Wall Street branch of the United States Bank.

In 1987, the three-story Lila Acheson Wallace Wing opened housing the Met's collection of contemporary art. Pablo Picasso's 1906 portrait of Gertrude Stein is the centerpiece of this collection.

There is much more to the Met than paintings, however. Visitors with a taste for classical art should go immediately to the left of the Great Hall on the first floor to see the Greek and Roman statuary. The Met's awesome Egyptian collection, spanning some 3,000 years, lies on the first floor directly to the right of the Great Hall. Its centerpiece is the Temple of Dendụr, an entire Roman-period temple (circa 15 BC) donated by the Egyptian government in thanks for U.S. help in saving ancient monuments.

Although it exhibits only a portion of its vast holdings, the Met offers more than can reasonably be seen in one visit. Choose what you want to see, find a map, and plan your tour accordingly. Walking tours and lectures are free with your contribution for admittance. Tours covering various sections of the museum begin about every 15 minutes on weekdays, less frequently on weekends; they depart from the Tour Board in the Great Hall. Self-guided audio tours can also be rented at a desk in the Great Hall. Lectures, often related to temporary exhibitions, are given frequently. *5th Ave. at 82nd St., ☎ 212/535–7710. Suggested contribution: $7 adults, $3.50 students and senior citizens. ☉ Tues.–Thurs. and Sun. 9:30–5:15, Fri. and Sat. 9:30–8:45.*

❹ Frank Lloyd Wright's **Guggenheim Museum** (opened in 1959) is a controversial work of architecture—even many of those who like its assertive six-story spiral rotunda will admit that it does not result in the best space in which to view art. Inside, under a 92-foot-high glass dome, a quarter-mile-long ramp spirals down past changing exhibitions of modern art. The museum has especially strong holdings in Wassily Kandinsky, Paul Klee, and Pablo Picasso; the oldest pieces are by the French Impressionists. *1071 5th Ave., at 88th St., ☎ 212/423–3500. ☛ $7 adults, $4 students and senior citizens. ☉ Sun.–Wed. 10–6, Fri. and Sat. 10–8.*

❺ A block north is the **National Academy of Design,** housed in a stately 19th-century mansion and a pair of town houses on 89th Street. The academy itself, which was founded in 1825, required each elected member to donate a representative work of art, which has resulted in a strong collection of 19th-and 20th-century American art. (Members have included Mary Cassatt, Samuel F. B. Morse, Winslow

Homer, John Singer Sargent, Frank Lloyd Wright, and Robert Rauschenberg.) *1083 5th Ave. at 89th St., ☎ 212/369–4880. ☛ $3.50 adults, $2 students, senior citizens and children under 16 free Fri. 5–8. ☉ Wed.–Sun. noon–5, Fri. noon–8.*

⑥ At 91st Street you'll find the former residence of industrialist Andrew Carnegie, now the home of the **Cooper-Hewitt Museum** (officially the Smithsonian Institution's National Museum of Design). Carnegie sought comfort more than show when he built this 64-room house on what were the outskirts of town in 1901; he administered his extensive philanthropic projects from the first-floor study. The core of the museum's collection was begun in 1897 by the three Hewitt sisters, granddaughters of inventor and industrialist Peter Cooper; major holdings include drawings, prints, textiles, furniture, metalwork, ceramics, glass, woodwork, and wall coverings. *2 E. 91st St., ☎ 212/860–6868. ☛ $3 adults, $1.50 students and senior citizens; free Tues. 5–9. ☉ Tues. 10–9, Wed.–Sat. 10–5, Sun. noon–5.*

⑦ The **Jewish Museum** opened its expanded and renovated facilities in June 1993. The expansion preserved the gray stone Gothic-style 1908 mansion occupied by the museum since 1947 and enlarged the 1963 addition. At the same time, the mansion facade was extended, giving the museum the appearance of a late–French Gothic château. The permanent two-floor exhibition, presented alongside temporary shows, traces the development of Jewish culture and identity over 4,000 years. *1109 5th Ave. at 92nd St., ☎ 212/423–3230. ☛ $6 adults, $4 students and senior citizens. Pay what you wish Tues. after 5. ☉ Sun., Mon., Wed., Thurs. 11–5:45; Tues. 11–8. Closed national and Jewish holidays.*

The handsome, well-proportioned Georgian-style mansion on the corner of 5th Avenue and 94th Street was built in 1914 for Willard Straight, founder of the *New Republic* mag-
⑧ azine. Today it is the home of the **International Center of Photography** (ICP), a relatively young institution—founded in 1974—building a strong collection of 20th-century photography. Its changing exhibitions often focus on the work of a single prominent photographer or one photographic

genre (portraits, architecture, etc.). *1130 5th Ave. at 94th St., ☎ 212/860–1777. ☛ $4 adults, $2.50 students and senior citizens, $1 children under 12. Pay what you wish Tues. 6–8. ⊙ Tues. 11–8, Wed.–Sun. 11–6.*

⑨ The Museum of the City of New York traces the course of Big Apple history, from the Dutch settlers of Nieuw Amsterdam to the present day, with period rooms, dioramas, slide shows, and clever displays of memorabilia. Weekend programs appeal especially to children. *5th Ave. at 103rd St., ☎ 212/534–1672. Suggested contribution: $5 adults; $3 students, senior citizens, and children; $8 families. ⊙ Wed.–Sat. 10–5, Sun. 1–5; closed Mon. and holidays, Tues. open for tour groups only.*

⑩ El Museo del Barrio, founded in 1969, concentrates on Latin culture in general, with a particular emphasis on Puerto Rican art. ("El Barrio" means "the neighborhood," and the museum is positioned on the edge of Spanish Harlem.) The 8,000-object permanent collection includes numerous pre-Columbian artifacts. *1230 5th Ave. at 104th St., ☎ 212/831–7272. Suggested contribution: $4 adults, $2 students and senior citizens. ⊙ Wed.–Sun. 11–5; Thurs. May–Sept. noon–7.*

Having completed this long walk, you may want to reward
⑪ yourself by crossing the street to Central Park's **Conservatory Garden.** The entrance, at 105th Street, is through elaborate wrought-iron gates that once graced the mansion of Cornelius Vanderbilt II. In contrast to the deliberately rustic effect of the rest of the park, this is a symmetrical, formal garden. To the south is a high-hedged flower garden named after Frances Hodgson Burnett, author of the children's classic *The Secret Garden.*

Tour 6: Central Park

Numbers in the margin correspond to points of interest on the Museum Mile and Central Park map.

It's amazing that 843 acres of the world's most valuable real estate should be set aside as a park, yet the city's 1856 decision to do so has proved to be marvelous wisdom, for
★ Central Park contributes mightily toward helping New

Yorkers maintain their sanity. It provides space large enough to get lost in (the entire principality of Monaco would fit within its borders), space where you can escape from the rumble of traffic to hear a bird sing or watch an earthworm burrow into the soil.

Although it appears to be simply a swath of rolling countryside exempted from urban development, Central Park is in fact one of the most cunningly planned artificial landscapes ever built. When they began in 1858, designers Frederick Law Olmsted and Calvert Vaux were presented with a swampy neighborhood of a few farms, houses, and a church. It took them 16 years, $14 million, and 5 million cubic yards of moved earth to create this playground of lush lawns, thick forests, and quiet ponds. Hills and tunnels artfully conceal transverse roads (65th, 79th, 86th, and 97th streets) so crosstown traffic will not disturb park goers, and a meandering circular drive carries vehicular traffic in the park. The drive is closed to auto traffic on weekdays 10 AM–3 PM and 7–10 PM, and weekends and holidays.

Today Central Park hosts just about any activity that a city dweller might engage in outdoors: jogging, cycling, horseback riding, softball, ice skating, roller skating, croquet, tennis, bird-watching, boating, chess, checkers, theater, concerts, skateboarding, and folk dancing. Try to come on a weekend, when local residents gratefully flock here to play—free entertainment is on tap, and the entire social microcosm is on parade.

Weekend crowds also make it safe to go into virtually any area of the park, although even on weekdays you should be safe anywhere along this tour. Despite its bad reputation, Central Park has the lowest crime rate of any precinct in the city—though the wisest course is to stay out of it at night (unless you are attending a free concert along with thousands of others).

At Grand Army Plaza, or most intersections of Central Park South (59th Street's name between 5th and 8th avenues), you can hire a ride in a horse-drawn carriage through the park. The official rates are $35 for each half hour, although drivers may try to get more, so agree on a price in advance. By the way: You can charge the ride to an American Express card.

To explore the park on foot, begin at Grand Army Plaza. Enter the park along the main road (East Drive), turning

⑫ down the first path to your left to the **Pond.** Walk along the shore to the Gapstow Bridge (each of the park's 30 bridges has its own name and individual design), where you can look back at the often-photographed view of midtown skyscrapers reflected in the pond.

⑬ Return to the main path and continue north to **Wollman Memorial Rink,** an ice-skating throughout the winter, a rollerblading and miniature golf spot from April through October. Even if you don't want to join in, you can stand on the terrace here to watch. ☎ 212/517–4800. ☛ $6.50 adults, $3.25 children under 13. Skate rental: $3.25. ☉ Mon., Wed., Thurs. 10–9:30; Tues. 10–5; Fri., Sat. 10–11.

From April through October part of the rink becomes the **Gotham Miniature Golf** course, where putters maneuver around scale models of various city landmarks. ☎ 212/517–4800. ☛ $6.50 adults, $3.50 children under 13. ☉ Mon. 10–5, Tues.–Thurs. 10–9:30, Fri. and Sat. 10 AM–11 PM, Sun. 10–9:30.

⑭ The 15 grassy acres of the **Sheep Meadow** make an ideal spot for picnicking or sunbathing. It's an officially designated quiet zone, where the most vigorous sports allowed are kite-flying and Frisbee-tossing. This lawn was actually used for grazing sheep until 1934; the nearby sheepfold was turned into the Tavern on the Green restaurant (see Tour 7, below).

The 72nd Street transverse—the only crosstown street that connects with the East, Center, and West drives—cuts across the park just north of here, but you can cross it or pass beneath it through a lovely tiled arcade to reach

⑮ **Bethesda Fountain,** set on an elaborately patterned paved terrace on the edge of the **lake.** This ornate, three-tiered fountain is named after the biblical Bethesda pool in Jerusalem, which was supposedly given healing powers by an angel (hence the angel rising from the center). Perch on the low terrace wall or the edge of the fountain and watch the rowboaters stroke past on the lake. If you want to get out on the water yourself, take the path east from the ter-

⑯ race to **Loeb Boathouse,** where in season you can rent a rowboat. The boathouse also operates a bike-rental facility and a better-than-average restaurant. *Boat rental $10 per hr, $20 deposit; ☎ 212/517–4723. Bicycle rental $6 per hr, tandems $12 per hr; ☎ 212/861–4137. ⊙ May–Oct., daily 11–6.*

⑰ The path to the west of the terrace leads to **Bow Bridge,** a splendid cast-iron bridge arching over a neck of the lake. The view from either side is postcard-perfect, with the water reflecting a quintessentially New York image of vintage apartment buildings peeping above the treetops. If **⑱** you continue across the bridge, you'll enter the **Ramble,** a heavily wooded 37-acre area laced with twisting, climbing paths. This is prime bird-watching territory; a rest stop along a major migratory route, it shelters many of the 269 species of birds that have been sighted in the park. Because it is so dense and isolated, however, it may not be a good place to wander alone.

If you backtrack to the 72nd Street traverse and head west, **⑲** you'll come to **Strawberry Fields,** the "international peace garden" memorializing John Lennon. Climbing up a hill, its curving paths, shrubs, trees, and flower beds create a deliberately informal pastoral landscape, reminiscent of the English parks Lennon may have been thinking of when he wrote the Beatles song "Strawberry Fields Forever" in 1967.

⑳ Vista Rock is dominated by **Belvedere Castle,** built in 1872 of the same gray Manhattan schist that thrusts out of the soil in dramatic outcrops throughout the park. The castle has been a measurement station of the U.S. Weather Bureau since 1919; look up to see the twirling meteorological instruments atop the tower. Climb out onto its balconies for a dramatic view, or get a minilesson in geology from the exhibits within. If you've got children with you, visit the ground-floor learning center. *☎ 212/772–0210. ☛ Free. ⊙ Mid-Feb.–mid-Oct. Tues.–Thurs. and weekends 11– 5, Fri. 1–5; Mid-Oct.–mid-Feb., closes at 4 PM.*

㉑ Just past the clock is the **Central Park Zoo,** recently renamed the **Central Park Wildlife Conservation Center,** a small but delightful menagerie. Clustered around the central Sea Lion Pool are separate exhibits for each of the earth's major environments; even a leisurely visit will take only about an hour, for there are only about 100 species on display. ☎ 212/439–6500. ☛ *$2.50 adults, $1.25 senior citizens, 50¢ children 3–12. No children under 16 allowed in without adult.* ☉ *Apr.–Oct., Mon. and Wed.–Fri. 10–4:30, Tues. 10–7, weekends and holidays 10–5; Nov.–Mar., daily 10–4.*

Tour 7: The Upper West Side

Numbers in the margin correspond to points of interest on the Upper West Side map.

The Upper West Side has never been as fashionable as the East Side, despite the fact that it has a similar mix of real estate—large apartment buildings along Central Park West, West End Avenue, and Riverside Drive, and town houses on the shady, quiet cross streets. Once a haven for the Jewish intelligentsia, the West Side had become by the 1960s a rather grungy multiethnic community. A slow process of gentrification began in the 1970s, however, when actors, writers, and gays began to move into the area. Today this neighborhood has become quite desirable, with lots of restored brownstones and high-priced co-op apartments.

❶ The West Side story begins at **Columbus Circle,** where a statue of Christopher himself crowns a stately pillar at the intersection of Broadway, 8th Avenue, Central Park West, and Central Park South. Columbus Circle is a good place to begin any tour of New York, for it is the headquarters of the **New York Convention and Visitors Bureau,** in a weird pseudo-Byzantine structure, ostensibly modeled after the Doge's Palace in Venice but locally nicknamed the Lollipop Building. Count on the bureau for brochures; bus and subway maps; hotel, restaurant, and shopping guides; a seasonal calendar of events; free TV-show tickets (sometimes) and discounts on Broadway theater; and sound advice. *2 Columbus Circle,* ☎ *212/397–8222.* ☉ *Weekdays 9–6, weekends and holidays 10–3.*

❷ New York's major site for the performing arts: **Lincoln Center,** covers an eight-block area west of Broadway between 62nd and 66th streets. This unified complex of pale travertine marble was built during the 1960s to supplant an urban ghetto (*West Side Story* was filmed on the slum's gritty,

American Museum of Natural History, **5**

Barnard College, **9**

Cathedral of St. John the Divine, **7**

Columbia University, **8**

Columbus Circle, **1**

The Dakota, **4**

Grant's Tomb, **10**

Hayden Planetarium, **5**

Lincoln Center, **2**

Museum of American Folk Art, **3**

Riverside Church, **11**

Riverside Park, **6**

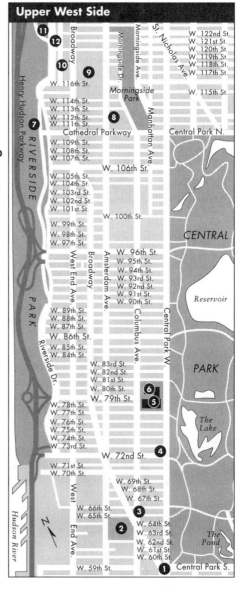

Upper West Side

deserted streets just before the demolition crews moved in). Lincoln Center can seat nearly 18,000 spectators at one time in its various halls (*see* Chapter 6).

Stand on Broadway, facing the central court with its huge fountain. The three concert halls on this plaza clearly relate to one another architecturally, with their symmetrical bilevel facades, yet each has slightly different lines and different details. To your left, huge honeycomb lights hang on the portico of the **New York State Theater,** home to the New York City Ballet and the New York City Opera. Straight ahead, at the rear of the plaza, is the **Metropolitan Opera House,** its brilliant-colored Chagall tapestries visible through the arched lobby windows; the Metropolitan Opera and American Ballet Theatre perform here. To your right, abstract bronze sculptures distinguish **Avery Fisher Hall,** host to the New York Philharmonic Orchestra.

Wander through the plaza, then veer to your left between the New York State Theater and the Metropolitan Opera House into **Damrosch Park,** where summer open-air festivals are often accompanied by free concerts at the **Guggenheim Bandshell.** Angle to your right from the plaza, between the Metropolitan and Avery Fisher, and you'll come to the North Plaza, with a massive Henry Moore sculpture reclining in a reflecting pool.

An overpass leads from this plaza across 65th Street to the world-renowned **Juilliard School** (for music and theater). Check here to see if there's a concert or a play going on; actors Kevin Kline and Patti LuPone once performed here. Turn left from the overpass and follow the walkway west to Lincoln Center's newest arts venue, the **Walter Reade Theater,** opened in the fall of 1991, showing several unusual American and foreign films a day, seven days a week (*see* Chapter 6).

Visitors can wander freely through the lobbies of all these buildings. One-hour guided "Introduction to Lincoln Center" tours, given daily, cover the center's history and wealth of artworks and usually visit the three principal theaters, performance schedules permitting. ☎ *212/875–5350 for schedule and reservations.* ☛ *$7.75 adults, $6.75 students and senior citizens, $4.50 children 6–12.*

❸ Across the busy intersection, the **Museum of American Folk Art** has found a new home at Columbus Avenue and 66th Street. Its collection includes naïve paintings, quilts, carvings, dolls, trade signs, painted wood carousel horses, and a giant Indian-chief copper weathervane. *2 Lincoln Sq.,* ☎ *212/977–7298. Suggested contribution: $2.* ☉ *Tues.–Sun. 11:30–7:30.*

Just inside Central Park at 66th Street is another dining landmark, **Tavern on the Green** (*see* Chapter 4). Originally built as a sheepfold, in the days when sheep grazed on the meadows of the park, it was converted into a restaurant in the 1930s. True, the high tone is not what it once was, but many of its dining rooms have fine park views; at night white lights strung through the surrounding trees create a magical effect.

❹ Continue up Central Park West to 72nd Street, where the stately **Dakota** presides over the northwest corner. Its tenants have included Rudolf Nureyev, Lauren Bacall, Rex Reed, and Gilda Radner. Resembling a buff-colored castle, with copper turrets, its slightly spooky appearance was played up in the movie *Rosemary's Baby,* which was filmed here. Stop by the gate on 72nd Street; this is the spot where, in December 1980, a deranged fan shot John Lennon as he came home from a recording session. Lennon is memorialized in Central Park's Strawberry Fields, across the street (*see* Tour 6, *above*).

Proceed up Central Park West and you'll see several other famous apartment buildings, including **The Langham** (135 Central Park West), where Mia Farrow's apartment was featured in Woody Allen's film *Hannah and Her Sisters;* and the twin-towered **San Remo** (145–146 Central Park West), over the years home to Rita Hayworth, Dustin Hoffman, Raquel Welch, Paul Simon, Barry Manilow, and Tony Randall—but not to Madonna, whose application was rejected because of her flamboyant lifestyle.

★ **❺** The **American Museum of Natural History,** the attached **Hayden Planetarium,** and their surrounding grounds occupy a four-block tract bounded by Central Park West, Columbus Avenue, and 77th and 81st streets. As you approach at 77th Street, you can see the original architecture in the pink granite corner towers, with their beehive crowns. A more classical facade was added along Central Park West, with its centerpiece an enormous equestrian statue of President Theodore Roosevelt, naturalist and explorer. In 1995, the museum celebrated its 125th birthday.

With a collection of more than 30 million artifacts, the museum displays something for every taste, from a 94-foot blue whale to the 563-carat Star of India sapphire. Among the most enduringly popular exhibits are the wondrously detailed dioramas of animal habitat groups, on the first and second floors just behind the rotunda, and the fourth-floor halls full of dinosaur skeletons. A five-story-tall cast of Barosaurus rears on its hind legs in the Roosevelt Rotunda, protecting its fossilized baby from a fossil allosaur. The Hall of Human Biology and Evolution investigates the workings of the human body and features a computerized archaeological dig and an electronic newspaper about human evolution. The Naturemax Theater projects films on a giant screen; the Hayden Planetarium (on 81st Street) has two stories of exhibits, plus several different Sky Shows projected on 22 wraparound screens; its rock-music laser shows draw crowds of teenagers on Friday and Saturday nights. *Museum:* ☎ *212/769–5100. Suggested contribution: $6 adults, $4 seniors and students, $3 children.* ☉ *Sun.–Thurs. 10–5:45; Fri.–Sat. 10–8:45. Planetarium:* ☎ *212/769– 5920.* ☛ *$5 adults, $4 senior citizens and students; $2.50 children 2–12; $8.50 for laser show.* ☉ *Weekdays 12:30– 4:45, Sat. 10–5:45, Sun. noon–5:45. Naturemax Theater film* ☛ *$6 adults, $5 senior citizens and students, $3 children under 13. Call 212/769–5650 for show times.*

TIME OUT For a diner-style lunch of a cheeseburger and banana split, stop by **EJ's Luncheonette** (447 Amsterdam Ave., ☎ 212/ 873-3444). If it's a nice day, another option is to pop into any deli and take your sandwiches and sodas one block over to sit in Central Park.

Return to Broadway to join New Yorkers in a pilgrimage to one of the city's greatest food shrines—**Zabar's** (between 80th and 81st Sts.)—which offers exquisite delicatessen items, prepared foods, gourmet groceries, coffee, and cheeses; a mezzanine level features cookware, dishes, and small appliances. Be prepared to muscle a lot of pushy strangers for elbow room, for Zabar's prides itself on carrying a vast range of hard-to-get foods, and at prices that are reasonable.

If you're up for a movie, about 10 blocks down is the new **Sony Imax Theater** (1998 Broadway, between 67th and 68th Sts., ☎ 212/336–5000), a massive complex that screens 3-D films on 8-story-high screens. Plastic headsets with infrared sensors are available to enhance your viewing pleasure.

❻ Having bought your picnic lunch, you may now want to head west to **Riverside Park,** a long, slender green space along the Hudson River landscaped by Central Park architects Olmsted and Vaux. Beginning at about 80th Street is the **Promenade,** a broad formal walkway with a stone parapet looking out over the river. Descend the steps here and go through the underpass beneath Riverside Drive, to reach the **79th Street Boat Basin,** a rare spot in Manhattan where you can walk right along the river's edge, smell the salt air, and watch a flotilla of houseboats bob in the water.

★ ❼ Take a cab or the Amsterdam Avenue bus up 112th Street and stop at the **Cathedral of St. John the Divine,** New York's major Episcopal church. When it is completed, it will be the largest cathedral in the world (St. Peter's of Rome is larger, but it's technically a basilica). Here you can have a rare, fascinating look at a Gothic cathedral in progress. Its first cornerstone was laid in 1892 and a second in 1925, but with the U.S. entry into World War II, construction came to a "temporary" halt that lasted until 1982. St. John's follows traditional Gothic engineering—it is supported by stonemasonry rather than by a steel skeleton—so new stonecutters, many of them youngsters from nearby Harlem neighborhoods, had to be trained before the current work could proceed. A model in the superb gift shop inside shows what the cathedral might look like when completed, probably quite a few years into the future.

Inside is a vast nave, the length of two football fields, which can seat 5,000 worshipers. The second chapel to your left is the only **Poets' Corner** in the United States; the right-hand aisle's chapels movingly mourn tragedies such as the

Holocaust and the spread of AIDS. *1047 Amsterdam Ave. at 112th St.,* ☎ *212/316–7540 or 212/662–2133 for box office. Suggested contribution: $2. Tours Tues.–Sat. 11, Sun. 1.* ☉ *Daily 7–5; Sun. to 8 PM.*

At 116th Street and Amsterdam, you can pass through the campus gates of **Columbia University,** a wealthy, private, coed institution that is New York City's only Ivy League school. The gilded crowns on the black wrought-iron gates serve as a reminder that this was originally King's College when it was founded in 1754, before American independence. Walk along the herringbone-patterned brick paths of College Walk into the refreshingly green main quadrangle, dominated by massive neoclassical **Butler Library** to your left (south) and the rotunda-topped **Low Memorial Library** to your right (north). Butler, built in 1934, holds the bulk of the university's 5-million books; Low, built in 1895–97 by McKim, Mead & White (who laid out the general campus plan when the college moved here in 1897), is now mostly offices, but on weekdays you can go inside to see its domed, templelike former Reading Room. Low Library also houses the visitor center, where you can pick up a campus guide or arrange a tour.

Across Broadway from Columbia is its sister institution, **Barnard College,** established in 1889. One of the former Seven Sisters of women's colleges, Barnard has steadfastly remained a single-sex institution and has maintained its independence from Columbia, although its students can take classes there (and vice versa). Note the bear (the college's mascot) on the shield above the main gates at 117th Street.

Across Riverside Drive, in Riverside Park, stands the immense **Grant's Tomb,** where Civil War general and two-term president Ulysses S. Grant rests beside his wife, Julia Dent Grant. The white granite mausoleum, with its imposing columns and classical pediment, is modeled after Les Invalides in Paris, where Napoléon is buried. Under a small white dome, the Grants' twin black marble sarcophagi are sunk into a deep circular chamber, which you view from above; minigalleries to the sides display photographs and Grant memorabilia. In contrast to this austere monument, the surrounding plaza features fanciful 1960s-era mosaic benches, designed by local schoolchildren. *Riverside Dr. and 122nd St.,* ☎ *212/666–1640.* ☛ *Free.* ⊗ *Wed.–Sun. 9–4:30.*

Just south of Grant's Tomb, on Riverside Drive at 120th
⑪ Street, **Riverside Church** is a modern (1930) Gothic-style edifice whose smooth, pale limestone walls seem the antithesis of St. John the Divine's rough gray hulk; in fact, it feels more akin to Rockefeller Center, not least because John D. Rockefeller was a major benefactor of the church. Inside, look at the handsomely ornamented main sanctuary, which seats only half as many people as St. John the Divine does. ☎ *212/222–5900.* ⊗ *Mon.–Sat. 9–5, Sun. noon–4; service each Sun. 10:45.*

Tour 8: Greenwich Village

Numbers in the margin correspond to points of interest on the Greenwich Village map.

Greenwich Village, which New Yorkers almost invariably speak of simply as "the Village," enjoyed a raffish reputation for years. Originally a rural outpost of the city—a haven for New Yorkers during early 19th-century smallpox and yellow fever epidemics—many of its blocks still look somewhat pastoral, with brick town houses and low rises; tiny green parks and hidden courtyards; and a crazy-quilt pattern of narrow, tree-lined streets. In the mid-19th century, however, as the city spread north of 14th Street, the Village became the province of immigrants, bohemians, and students (New York University, today the nation's largest private university, was planted next to Washington Square in 1831). Its politics were radical and its attitudes tolerant, which is one reason it is now home to such a large gay community. Today Village apartments and town houses go for high rents, and several posh restaurants have put down roots. Except for the isolated western fringe, where a string of tough gay bars along West Street attracts some drug traffic and prostitution, the Village is about as safe and clean as the Upper East Side. The Village is no longer dangerous, but it still feels bohemian.

Several generations of writers and artists have lived and worked here: in the 19th century, Henry James, Edgar

Allan Poe, and Walt Whitman; at the turn of the century, O. Henry, Edith Wharton, and Hart Crane; and during the 1920s and '30s, John Dos Passos, Norman Rockwell, Sinclair Lewis, and Edna St. Vincent Millay. In the late 1940s and early 1950s, the Abstract Expressionist painters Franz Kline, Jackson Pollock, Mark Rothko, and Willem de Kooning congregated here, as did the Beat writers Jack Kerouac, Allen Ginsberg, and Lawrence Ferlinghetti. The 1960s brought folk musicians and poets, notably Bob Dylan and Peter, Paul, and Mary.

❶ Washington Square Begin a tour of Greenwich Village at Washington Arch in **Washington Square** at the foot of 5th Avenue. Designed by Stanford White, a wood version of Washington Arch was built in 1889 to commemorate the 100th anniversary of George Washington's presidential inauguration and was originally placed about half a block north of its present location. The arch was reproduced in stone in 1892, and the statues—*Washington at War* on the left, *Washington at Peace* on the right—were added in 1913.

Washington Square started out as a cemetery, principally for yellow-fever victims, and an estimated 10,000–22,000 bodies lie below. In the early 1800s it was a parade ground and the site of public executions; bodies dangled from a conspicuous Hanging Elm that still stands at the northwest corner of the square. Later Washington Square became the focus of a fashionable residential neighborhood and a center of outdoor activity.

Most of the buildings bordering Washington Square belong to New York University. **The Row,** a series of beautifully preserved Federal-style town houses along Washington Square North between 5th Avenue and University Place, now serves as university offices and faculty housing. Developers were not so tactful when they demolished 18 Washington Square, once the home of Henry James's grandmother, which he later used as the setting for his novel *Washington Square* (Henry himself was born just off the square, in a long-gone house on Washington Place). The house at 20 Washington Square North is the oldest building (1820) on the block. Notice its Flemish bond brickwork—alternate bricks inserted with the smaller surface (headers) facing out—

Greenwich Village

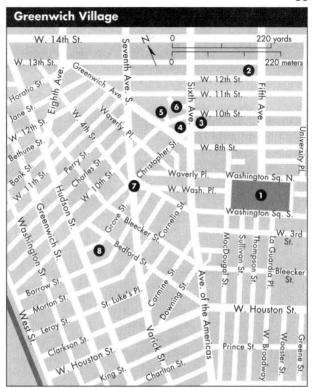

which before 1830 was considered the best way to build stable walls.

Go up 5th Avenue half a block to **Washington Mews,** a cobblestone private street lined on one side with the former stables of the houses on the Row. Writer Walter Lippmann and artist-patron Gertrude Vanderbilt Whitney (founder of the Whitney Museum) once had homes in the mews; today it's mostly owned by NYU. A similar Village mews, **MacDougal Alley,** can be found between 8th Street and the square just off MacDougal Street, one block west.

Walk up 5th Avenue, past the **Church of the Ascension** (5th Ave. and W. 10th St.), a Gothic-style brownstone designed by Richard Upjohn. Inside, you can admire a mural depicting the Ascension of Jesus and stained-glass windows by John LaFarge and a marble altar sculpture by Louis Saint-Gaudens. In 1844, President John Tyler married Julia Gardiner **❷** here. Just past 12th Street, you can stop in the **Forbes Magazine Galleries,** where the late publisher Malcolm Forbes's idiosyncratic personal collection is on display. Exhibits change in the large gallery while permanent highlights include U.S. presidential papers, more than 500 intricate model boats, 12 jeweled Fabergé eggs, and some 12,000 toy soldiers. *62 5th Ave. at 12th St.,* ☎ *212/206–5548.* ☛ *Free.* ☉ *Tues.–Wed. and Fri.–Sat. 10–4.*

Backtrack on 5th Avenue to **West 11th Street** and turn right to see one of the best examples of a Village town-house block. One exception to the general 19th-century redbrick look is the modern, angled front window of 18 West 11th Street, usually occupied by a stuffed bear whose outfit changes from day to day. This house was built after the original was destroyed in a 1970 explosion; members of the radical Weathermen faction had started a bomb factory in the basement.

On Avenue of the Americas (6th Avenue), turn left to sam- **❸** ple the wares at **Balducci's** (6th Ave. and 9th St., ☎ 212/673–2600), a full-service gourmet food store that sprouted from the vegetable stand of the late Louis Balducci Sr. Along with more than 80 Italian cheeses and 50 kinds of bread, this family-owned enterprise features imported Italian specialties and a prodigious selection of fresh seafood.

Directly opposite, the triangle formed by West 10th Street, 6th Avenue, and Greenwich Avenue originally held a green-market, a jail, and the magnificent towered courthouse that ❹ is now the **Jefferson Market Library** (☎ 212/243–4334). Critics variously termed the courthouse's hodgepodge of styles Venetian, Victorian, or Italian; Villagers, noting the alternating wide bands of redbrick and narrow strips of granite, dubbed it the Lean Bacon Style. Over the years, the structure has housed a number of government agencies (public works, civil defense, census bureau, police academy); it was on the verge of demolition when public-spirited citizens saved it and turned it into a public library in 1967. Inside, look at the handsome interior doorways and climb the graceful circular stairway. If the gate is open, visit the flower garden behind the library, a project run by local green thumbs.

Just west of 6th Avenue on 10th Street is the wrought-iron ❺ gateway to a tiny courtyard called **Patchin Place;** around the corner, on 6th Avenue just north of 10th Street, is a sim- ❻ ilar cul-de-sac, **Milligan Place,** which few New Yorkers even know is there. Both were built around 1850 for the waiters (mostly Basques) who worked at the high-society Brevoort Hotel, long ago demolished, on 5th Avenue. Patchin Place later became home to several writers, including Theodore Dreiser, e. e. cummings, Eugene O'Neill, and Djuna Barnes.

Take Christopher Street, which veers off from the southern end of the library triangle, a few steps to **Gay Street.** A curved lane lined with small row houses circa 1810, Gay Street was originally a black neighborhood and later a strip of speakeasies. Ruth McKinney lived and wrote *My Sister Eileen* in the basement of No. 14, and Howdy Doody was designed in the basement of No. 12. At the end of Gay Street go west on Waverly Place to Christopher Street.

If you continue west on Christopher Street, you'll pass steps leading down to the **Lion's Head** (59 Christopher St.), a longtime hangout for literary types. Before she found stardom, Jessica Lange was a waitress here, and book covers by semiresident authors line the walls. The restaurant faces a green triangle that's technically called **Christopher Park,** but it contains a statue of Civil War general Philip

Sheridan; this confuses New Yorkers, because there's another triangle to the south (between Washington Place, Barrow Street, and 7th Avenue) called **Sheridan Square,** which was recently landscaped following an extensive dig by urban archaeologists, who unearthed artifacts dating back to the Dutch and Native American eras.

Sheridan Square was the site of a nasty 1863 riot in which a group of freed slaves was nearly lynched; in 1969, gays and police clashed nearby during a protest march that galvanized the gay-rights movement. Across the busy intersection of 7th Avenue, **Christopher Street** comes into its own as the symbolic heart of New York's gay community. Many bars and stores along here cater to that clientele, although the street is by no means off-limits to other people. The **Li-Lac Chocolate Shop** (120 Christopher St., ☎ 212/242–7374), a longtime favorite in the area for its homemade chocolate and buttercrunch is worth a visit.

West of 7th Avenue, the Village turns into a picture-book town of twisting, tree-lined streets, quaint houses, and tiny restaurants. Follow Grove Street from Sheridan Square west past the house where Thomas Paine died (59 Grove St.) and the boyhood home of poet Hart Crane (45 Grove St.).

At this point, you'll be close to the intersection of Grove and Bleecker streets. You may now choose to take a leisurely stroll along the portion of Bleecker Street that extends west of 7th Avenue from Grove to Bank Street, heading in the direction of Abingdon Square. This section of Bleecker Street is full of crafts and antiques shops, coffeehouses, and small restaurants.

If you choose to forego Bleecker Street, continue your walk west on Grove Street. The secluded intersection of Grove and Bedford streets seems to have fallen through a time warp into the 19th century. On the northeast corner stands one of the few remaining clapboard structures in the city (17 Grove St.); wood construction was banned as a fire hazard in 1822, the year it was built. The house has since served many functions; it housed a brothel during the Civil War. Behind it, at 102 Bedford Street, is **Twin Peaks,** an 1835 house that was rather whimsically altered in the 1920s, with stucco, half-timbers, and a pair of steep roof peaks added on.

❽ Grove Street curves in front of the iron gate of **Grove Court,** an enclave of brick-fronted town houses from the mid-1800s. Built originally as apartments for employees at neighborhood hotels, Grove Court used to be called Mixed Ale Alley because of the residents' propensity to pool beverages brought from work. It now houses a more affluent crowd: A town house here recently sold for $3 million.

Return along Washington Square South to MacDougal Street and turn right. The **Provincetown Playhouse** (133 MacDougal St., ☎ 212/477–5048) premiered many of Eugene O'Neill's plays. Louisa May Alcott wrote *Little Women* while living at 130–132 MacDougal Street.

TIME OUT The neighborhood's oldest coffeehouse is **Caffè Reggio** (119 MacDougal St., ☎ 212/475-9557), where an antique machine steams forth espresso and cappuccino. The tiny tables are close together, but the crowd usually makes for interesting eavesdropping.

At **Minetta Tavern** (113 MacDougal St., ☎ 212/475–3850), a venerable Village watering hole, turn right onto **Minetta Lane,** which leads to narrow **Minetta Street,** another former speakeasy alley. Both streets follow the course of Minetta Brook, which once flowed through this neighborhood and still bubbles deep beneath the pavement.

Tour 9: SoHo

Numbers in the margin correspond to points of interest on the SoHo, Little Italy, Chinatown map.

Today SoHo is virtually synonymous with a certain postmodern chic—an amalgam of black-clad artists, hip young Wall Streeters, track-lit loft apartments, hip art galleries, and restaurants with a minimalist approach to both food and decor. It's all very urban, very cool, very now. But 25 years ago, they were virtual wastelands. SoHo (so named because it is the district *South of Houston Street,* bounded by Broadway, Canal Street, and 6th Avenue) was described in a 1962 City Club of New York study as "commercial slum number one." It was saved by two factors: (1) preservationists discovered here the world's greatest concentration of cast-iron architecture and fought to prevent demolition; and (2) artists discovered the large, cheap, well-lit spaces that cast-iron buildings provide. At first it was technically illegal for artists to live in their loft studios, but so many did that eventually the zoning laws were changed to permit residence.

Perhaps the best introduction to these areas is a walk up Greene Street, where the block between Canal and Grand streets contains the longest continuous row of cast-iron buildings anywhere (Nos. 8–34 Greene St.). The architectural rage between 1860 and 1890, cast-iron buildings were popular because they did not require massive walls to bear the weight of the upper stories. With no need for load-bearing walls, these buildings were able to have more interior space and larger windows. They were also versatile, with various architectural elements produced from standardized molds to mimic any style—Italianate, Victorian Gothic, neo-Grecian, to name but a few visible in SoHo. Look, for example, at 28–30 Greene

❶ Street, an 1873 building nicknamed the **Queen of Greene Street.** Overlooking its obvious need for a paint job, notice how many decorative features have been applied: dormers, columns, window arches, and projecting central bays. Handsome as they are, these buildings were always commercial, containing stores and light manufacturing, principally textiles. Along this street notice the iron loading docks and the sidewalk vault covers studded with glass disks to let light into basement storage areas.

❷ At 72–76 Greene Street is the so-called **King of Greene Street,** a five-story Renaissance-style building that has a magnificent projecting porch with Corinthian columns. Today the King (now painted yellow) houses the **M-13** art gallery (☎ 212/925–3007) and **Bennison Fabrics,** an upscale fabric shop.

Take Prince Street west to Wooster Street, which, like a few other SoHo streets, still has its 19th-century pavement of Belgian blocks, a smoother successor to traditional cob-

❸ blestones. Start at the **Paula Cooper Gallery** (155 Wooster St., ☎ 674–0766), one of SoHo's oldest galleries. At 141 Wooster Street, one of several outposts of the DIA Art

❹ Foundation, you can visit the **New York Earth Room,** Walter de Maria's avant-garde 1977 artwork that consists of 140 tons of gently sculpted soil filling a second-floor gallery. ☎ 212/473–8072. ☛ *Free.* ⊘ *Wed.–Sat. noon–6. Closed Memorial Day–Labor Day.*

Across the street is the **Gagosian Gallery** (136 Wooster St., ☎ 212/228–2828), operated by prominent uptown dealer Larry Gagosian. The gallery's silver-and-glass front resembles a very wide garage door. The thought-provoking **A.I.R. Gallery** (40 Wooster St., between Broome and Grand Sts., ☎ 212/966–0799) has been focusing on the work of women artists since 1972.

West Broadway (which, somewhat confusingly, runs parallel to and four blocks west of regular Broadway) is SoHo's main drag, and on Saturday it can be crowded with smartly dressed uptowners and suburbanites who've come down for a little store- and gallery-hopping (*see* Chapter 3). In the block between Prince and Spring streets alone there are three major art stops: **420 West Broadway,** with six separate galleries including two of the biggest SoHo names, Leo Castelli (☎ 212/431–5160) and the Sonnabend Gallery (☎ 212/966–6160); the **Mary Boone Gallery** (417 W. Broadway ☎ 212/431–1818); and another excellent cluster of galleries at **415 West Broadway,** including the Witkin Gallery (☎ 212/925–5510) for photography. One block south, at **383 West Broadway,** OK Harris (☎ 212/431–3600) has its digs.

Go east to Broome Street and Broadway, where, on the northeast corner, you'll see the newly restored classic of the cast-iron genre, the **Haughwout Building** (488 Broadway), nicknamed the Parthenon of Cast Iron. Built in 1857 to house Eder Haughwout's china and glassware business, the exterior was inspired by a Venetian palazzo. Inside, it contained the world's first commercial passenger elevator, a steam-powered device invented by Elisha Graves Otis.

If you're visiting the area on a weekend, take a side trip one block south to the corner of Grand Street. The **SoHo Antiques Fair** draws about 100 dealers to sell clothing, toys, antiques, jewelry, and other flea-market fare weekend days 9–5.

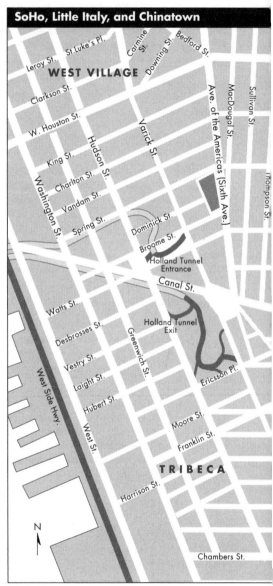

60

SoHo, Little Italy, and Chinatown

St. Luke's Pl.

Carmine St.

Downing St.

Bedford St.

Leroy St.

WEST VILLAGE

Clarkson St.

W. Houston St.

King St.

Charlton St.

Vandam St.

Spring St.

Hudson St.

Varick St.

Washington St.

MacDougal St.

Ave. of the Americas (Sixth Ave.)

Sullivan St.

Thompson St.

Dominick St.

Broome St.

Holland Tunnel Entrance

Canal St.

Watts St.

Desbrosses St.

Vestry St.

Laight St.

Hubert St.

Greenwich St.

Holland Tunnel Exit

Ericsson Pl.

West Side Hwy.

West St.

Moore St.

Franklin St.

TRIBECA

Harrison St.

N

Chambers St.

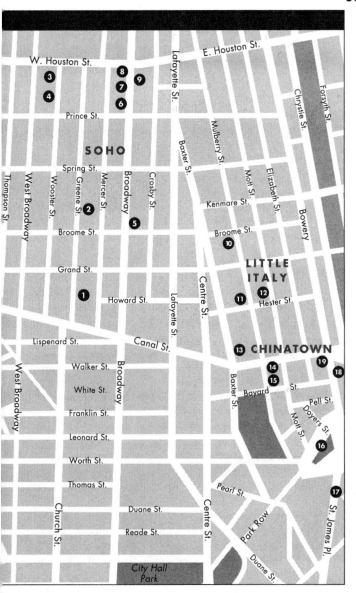

Head north up Broadway, which temporarily loses its SoHo ambience in the midst of discount clothing stores. Just below Prince Street, the 1907 **Singer Building** (561 Broadway) shows the final flower of the cast-iron style, with wrought-iron balconies, terra-cotta panels, and broad expanses of windows. Across the street is one of New York's gourmet shrines, the gleaming **Dean & DeLuca** food market (560 Broadway, ☎ 212/431–1691), whose bread and produce arrangements often are worthy of still-life paintings. The smartly restored **560 Broadway** building also houses a respected multigallery exhibit space.

6 On the west side of Broadway, the Guggenheim Museum opened a SoHo branch in 1992: the **Guggenheim Museum SoHo,** which displays a revolving series of exhibitions, both contemporary work and pieces from the Guggenheim's permanent collection. The museum occupies space in a landmark 19th-century redbrick structure with its original cast-iron storefronts and detailed cornice. Arata Isozaki designed the two floors of stark, loftlike galleries as well as the museum store facing West Broadway. *575 Broadway,* ☎ *212/423–3500.* ☛ *$5 adults, $3 senior citizens and students;* ☛ *higher for special exhibitions.* ☾ *Wed.–Fri. and Sun. 11–6, Sat. 11–8.*

7 A few doors up the street, the **New Museum of Contemporary Art** shows experimental, often radically innovative work—none of it more than 10 years old—by unrecognized artists. *583 Broadway,* ☎ *212/219–1222.* ☛ *$4 adults, $3 students, senior citizens, and artists.* ☾ *Wed., Thurs., Fri., and Sun. noon–6; Sat. noon–8.*

8 A few doors up the street (north) from the New Museum is the **Museum for African Art,** dedicated to contemporary and traditional African art. This fascinating addition to the SoHo scene is housed in a handsome, two-story space designed by Maya Lin, who also designed Washington, DC's Vietnam Veterans Memorial. Exhibits may include contemporary sculpture, ceremonial masks, architectural details, costumes, and textiles. *593 Broadway,* ☎ *212/966–1313.* ☛ *$4 adults; $2 students, senior citizens, and children under 12.* ☾ *Tues.–Fri. 10:30–5:30, weekends noon–6.*

9 Across Broadway, the **Alternative Museum,** a gallery that exhibits art with a political or sociopolitical twist, has moved up to SoHo from its former TriBeCa home. *594 Broadway,* ☎ *212/966–4444. Suggested contribution: $3.* ☯ *Tues.–Sat. 11–6.*

Tour 10: Little Italy

Numbers in the margin correspond to points of interest on the SoHo, Little Italy, Chinatown map.

Mulberry Street is the heart of Little Italy; in fact, at this point it's virtually the entire body. In 1932 an estimated 98% of the inhabitants of this area were of Italian birth or heritage, but since then the growth and expansion of neighboring Chinatown have encroached on the Italian neighborhood to such an extent that merchants and community leaders of the Little Italy Restoration Association (LIRA) negotiated a truce in which the Chinese agreed to let at least Mulberry remain an all-Italian street.

Start at the intersection of Spring and Mulberry streets, which still has a residential feel to it. The **D&G Bakery** (45 Spring St., ☎ 212/226–6688) is one of the last coal-oven bakeries in the United States. Buy a loaf of savory prosciutto bread, a meal in itself, with the Italian ham baked right into the bread. Walk down Mulberry Street to Broome Street, where the classic Little Italy really begins, crowded with restaurants, bakeries, imported-food shops, and souvenir stores.

At the southwest corner of Broome and Mulberry streets, stairs lead down through a glass entrance to what seems to be a blue-tiled cave—and, appropriately enough, it is the **10** **Grotta Azzurra** restaurant (387 Broome St., ☎ 212/925–8775), a longtime favorite for both the hearty food and the very Italian ambience.

At the corner of Mulberry and Grand streets, stop to get the lay of the land. Facing north (uptown), on your right you'll see a series of wide, four-story houses from the early 19th century, built long before the great flood of immigration hit this neighborhood between 1890 and 1924. Turn and look south along the east side of Mulberry Street to see Little Italy's predominant architecture today: tenement buildings with fire escapes projecting over the sidewalks. Most of these are of the late-19th-century New York style known as railroad flats: six-story buildings on 25-by-90-foot lots, with all the rooms in each apartment placed in a straight line like railroad cars. This style was common in the densely populated immigrant neighborhoods of lower Manhattan until 1901, when the city passed an ordinance requiring air shafts in the interior of buildings. On the southeast corner, **E. Rossi & Co.** (191 Grand St., ☎ 212/966–6640; established in 1902) is an antiquated little shop that sells housewares, espresso makers, embroidered religious postcards, and jocular Italian T-shirts. Down Grand Street is **Ferrara's** (195 Grand St., ☎ 212/226–6150), a 100-year-old pastry shop that ships its creations—cannoli, peasant pie, Italian rum cake—all over the world.

⓫ **Umberto's Clam House** (129 Mulberry St., ☎ 212/431–7545) is perhaps best known as the place where mobster Joey Gallo was munching scungili in 1973 when he was fatally surprised by a task force of mob hit men. Quite peaceful now, Umberto's specializes in fresh shellfish in a spicy tomato sauce. Turn onto Hester Street to visit yet another
⓬ Little Italy institution, **Puglia** (189 Hester St., ☎ 212/966–6006), a restaurant where guests sit at long communal tables, sing along with house entertainers, and enjoy moderately priced southern Italian specialties with quantities of homemade wine.

One street west, on Baxter Street about ¾ of a block to-
⓭ ward Canal Street, stands the **San Gennaro Church** (officially, Most Precious Blood Church, National Shrine of San Gennaro), which each year around September 19 sponsors Little Italy's keynote event, the annual Feast of San Gennaro. During the feasts, Little Italy's streets are closed to traffic, arches of tinsel span the thoroughfares, the sidewalks are lined with booths offering games and food, and the whole scene is one noisy, crowded, kitschy, delightful party.

Tour 11: Chinatown

Numbers in the margin correspond to points of interest on the SoHo, Little Italy, Chinatown map.

Visibly exotic, Chinatown is a popular tourist attraction, but it is also a real, vital community, where about half of the city's population of 300,000 Chinese still live. Its main businesses are restaurants and garment factories; some 55% of its residents speak little or no English. Theoretically, Chinatown is divided from Little Italy by Canal Street, the bustling artery that links the Holland Tunnel (to New Jersey) and the Manhattan Bridge (to Brooklyn). However, in recent years, an influx of immigrants from the People's Republic of China, Taiwan, and especially Hong Kong has swelled Manhattan's Chinese population, and Hong Kong residents, anticipating the return of the British colony to PRC domination in 1997, have been investing their capital in Chinatown real estate. Consequently, Chinatown now spills over its traditional borders into Little Italy to the north and the formerly Jewish Lower East Side to the east.

Originally Canal Street was a tree-lined road with a canal running its length. Today the Chinatown stretch of Canal Street is almost overwhelmed with sidewalk markets bursting with stacks of fresh seafood and strange-shaped vegetables in extraterrestrial shades of green. Food shops proudly display their wares: If America's motto is "a chicken in every pot," then Chinatown's must be "a roast duck in every window."

⑭ Kam Man (200 Canal St., ☎ 212/571–0330), a duplex supermarket, sells an amazing assortment of fresh and canned imported groceries, herbs, and the sort of dinnerware and furniture familiar to patrons of Chinese restaurants. Choose from dozens of varieties of noodles or such delicacies as dried starch and fresh chicken feet.

⑮ The **Chinatown History Museum,** at the corner of Bayard and Mulberry streets, shows interactive photographic exhibitions on Asian-American labor history. It also has a resource library and bookstore and offers a walking tour of Chinatown from April to November. *70 Mulberry St., 2nd Floor,* ☎ *212/619–4785.* ☛ *$1.* ⊘ *Weekdays and Sun. noon–5.*

Mott Street, the principal business street of the neighborhood, looks the way you might expect Chinatown to look: narrow and twisting, crammed with souvenir shops and restaurants in funky pagoda-style buildings, crowded with pedestrians at all hours of the day or night. Within the few dense blocks of Chinatown, hundreds of restaurants serve every imaginable type of Chinese cuisine, from fast-food noodles or dumplings to sumptuous Hunan, Szechuan, Cantonese, Mandarin, and Shanghai feasts. Every New Yorker thinks he or she knows the absolute, flat-out best, but whichever one you try, at 8 PM on Saturday, don't be surprised if you have to wait in line to get in.

Take a right on Mott Street and take a peek down Pell Street, a narrow lane of wall-to-wall restaurants whose neon signs stretch halfway across the thoroughfare. At 35 Pell Street is **May May Chinese Gourmet Bakery** (☎ 212/267–6733), a good place to stop for Chinese pastries, rice dumplings, and vegetarian specialties, such as yam cakes and vegetarian spring rolls.

TIME OUT   Turn right off Mott onto Bayard Street for the **Chinatown Ice Cream Factory** (65 Bayard St., between Mott and Elizabeth, ☎ 212/608–4170), a great spot for coconut, red-bean, or green-tea ice cream.

At the corner of Mott and Mosco streets stands the **Church of the Transfiguration.** Built in 1801 as the Zion Episcopal Church, this imposing Georgian structure with Gothic windows is now a Chinese Catholic church where mass is said in Cantonese, Mandarin, and English. Directly across the street from the church is **Quong Yuen Shing & Co.** (32 Mott St., ☎ 212/962–6280), also known as the Mott Street General Store, one of Chinatown's oldest curio shops, with porcelain bowls, teapots, and cups for sale.

⑯ At the end of Mott Street is **Chatham Square,** which is really more of a labyrinth than a square: 10 streets converge here, creating pandemonium for cars and a nightmare for pedestrians. A memorial, the **Kim Lau Arch,** honoring Chinese casualties in American wars, stands on an island in the eye of the storm.

Return to Chatham Square, cross Park Row (on your right) and take a sharp right turn on St. James Place to find two remnants of this neighborhood's pre-Chinatown past. On
⑰ St. James Place is the **First Shearith Israel graveyard.** The

first Jewish cemetery in the United States, this site was consecrated in 1656, when it was considered to be well outside of town.

⑱ Go back past Chatham Square and up the Bowery to **Confucius Plaza,** the open area at the intersection of Bowery and Division Street monitored by a statue of Confucius and the sweeping curve of a redbrick high-rise apartment complex named for him. At 18 Bowery, at the corner of Pell Street, stands one of Manhattan's oldest homes, a Federal and Georgian structure built in 1785 by meat wholesaler Edward Mooney. A younger side of Chinatown is shown at the

⑲ **Asian American Arts Centre,** which displays current work by Asian-American artists. There's no sign out front and the door reads KTV-City; ring buzzer No. 1. *26 Bowery,* ☏ *212/233–2154.* ☛ *Free.* ☉ *Tues.–Fri. noon–6, Sat. 1–3.*

For some exotic shopping, duck into the **Canal Arcade,** a passage that links the Bowery and Elizabeth Street. A few doors down, at 50 Bowery, you'll see the **Silver Palace** restaurant, worth a peek inside for its Chinese rococo interior, complete with dragons whose eyes are blinking lights.

Tour 12: Lower Manhattan

Numbers in the margin correspond to points of interest on the Lower Manhattan map.

Lower Manhattan doesn't cover many acres, but it is packed with attractions, for it has always been central to the city's networks of power and wealth. It was here that the Nieuw Amsterdam colony was established by the Dutch in 1625; in 1789, the first capital building of the United States was located here. The city did not really expand beyond these precincts until the middle of the 19th century. Today Lower Manhattan is in many ways dominated by Wall Street, which is both an actual street and a shorthand name for the vast, powerful financial community that clusters around the New York and American stock exchanges.

❶ To the west of South Ferry lies **Battery Park,** a verdant landfill loaded with monuments and sculpture, at Manhattan's green toe. The park's name refers to a line of cannons once

Alexander
Hamilton
Customs
House, **5**
Battery Park, **1**
Brooklyn
Bridge, **15**
Castle Clinton, **2**
City Hall, **14**
Ellis Island, **4**
Federal Hall
National
Memorial, **8**
Fraunces
Tavern, **7**
New York Stock
Exchange, **9**
St. Paul's
Chapel, **11**
South Street
Seaport Historic
District, **12**
Statue of
Liberty, **3**
Trinity
Church, **10**
Vietnam Veterans
Memorial, **6**
Woolworth
Building, **13**
World Financial
Center, **17**
World Trade
Center, **16**

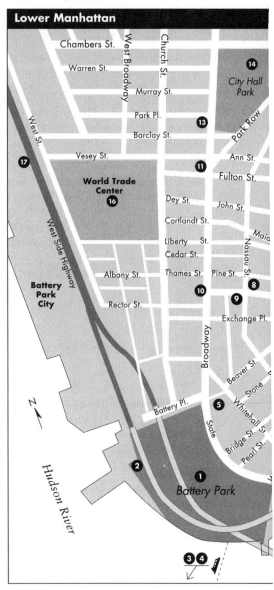

Lower Manhattan

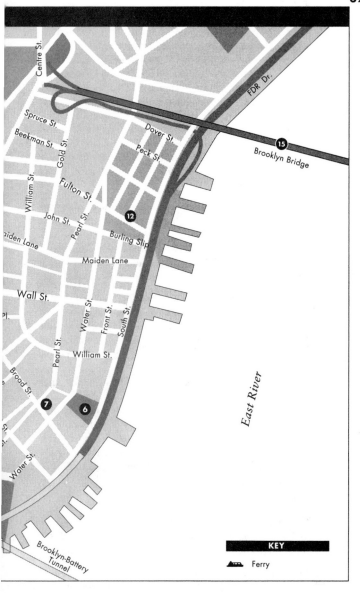

KEY

⚓ Ferry

mounted here to defend the shoreline (which ran along what is currently State Street). Head north along the water's edge to the **East Coast Memorial,** a statue of a fierce eagle that presides over eight granite slabs inscribed with the names of U.S. servicemen who died in the Western Atlantic during World War II. Climb the steps of the East Coast Memorial for a fine view of the main features of **New York Harbor;** from left to right: **Governors Island,** a Coast Guard installation; hilly **Staten Island** in the distance; the **Statue of Liberty** on Liberty Island; **Ellis Island,** gateway to the New World for generations of immigrants; and the old railway terminal in **Liberty State Park,** on the mainland in Jersey City, New Jersey.

Continue north past a romantic **statue of Giovanni da Verrazano,** the Florentine merchant who piloted the ship that first sighted New York and its harbor in 1524. The Verrazano-Narrows Bridge between Brooklyn and Staten Island—the world's longest suspension bridge—is visible from here, just beyond Governors Island.

② Built in 1811 as a defense for New York Harbor, the circular brick fortress now called **Castle Clinton** was, when first built, on an island 200 feet from shore. In 1824 it became Castle Garden, an entertainment and concert facility that reached its zenith in 1850 when more than 6,000 people (the capacity of Radio City Music Hall) attended the U.S. debut of the "Swedish Nightingale," Jenny Lind. After landfill connected it to the city, Castle Clinton became, in succession, an immigrant processing center, an aquarium, and now a restored fort, museum, and ticket office for ferries to the **Statue of Liberty** and **Ellis Island.** The ferry ride is one loop; you can get off at Liberty Island, visit the statue, then reboard any ferry and continue on to Ellis Island, boarding another boat once you have finished exploring the historic immigration facility there. *Ferry information: ☎ 212/269–5755. Round-trip fare: $7 adults, $5 senior citizens, $3 children 3–17. Departures every 45 min on weekdays and every 30 mins on weekends 9:30–3:30; more frequent departures and extended hours in summer.*

★ ③ After arriving on Liberty Island, you have two choices from the ground-floor entrance to the **Statue of Liberty** monument: you can take an elevator 10 stories to the top of the 89-foot-high pedestal, or if you're strong of heart and limb, you can climb 354 steps (the equivalent of a 22-story building) to the crown. (Visitors cannot go up into the torch.) It usually takes two to three hours to walk up to the crown because of the wait beforehand. Erected in 1886 and refurbished for its centennial, the Statue of Liberty weighs 225 tons and stands 151 feet from her feet to her torch. ☎ *212/363–3200 or 212/363–8340.* ☛ *Free.*

❹ The ferry's other stop, **Ellis Island,** opened in September 1990 to record crowds after a $140 million restoration. Now a national monument, Ellis Island was once a federal immigration facility that processed 17 million men, women, and children between 1892 and 1954—the ancestors of more than 40% of Americans living today. The island's main building contains the **Ellis Island Immigration Museum,** with exhibits detailing not only the island's history but the whole history of immigration to America. Perhaps the most moving exhibit is the American Immigrant Wall of Honor, where the names of nearly 400,000 immigrant Americans are inscribed along an outdoor promenade overlooking the Statue of Liberty and the Manhattan skyline. ☎ *212/363–3200; for Wall of Honor info,* ☎ *212/883–1986.* ☛ *Free.*

As you leave the park surrounding Castle Clinton, across State ❺ Street you'll see the imposing **Alexander Hamilton Custom House,** built in 1907 in the ornate Beaux Arts style fashionable at the time. Above the base, the facade features massive columns rising to a pediment topped by a double row of statuary. Daniel Chester French, better known for the statue of Lincoln in the Lincoln Memorial in Washington, DC, sculpted the lower statues, which symbolize various continents (left to right: Asia, the Americas, Europe, Africa); the upper row represents the major trading cities of the world. The Custom House is the home of the first national museum dedicated to Native American culture, the **National Museum of the American Indian.** The Smithsonian Institute's George Gustav Heye Center houses these well-mounted exhibits that examine the history and the current cultures of native peoples from all over the Americas through literature, dance, lectures, film, and crafts. *1 Bowling Green,* ☎ *212/668–6624.* ☛ *Free.* ☉ *Daily 10–5.*

The museum faces onto **Bowling Green,** an oval greensward at the foot of Broadway that became New York's first public park in 1733. On July 9, 1776, a few hours after citizens learned about the signing of the Declaration of Independence, rioters toppled a statue of British King George III that had occupied the spot for 11 years; much of the statue's lead was melted down into bullets. In 1783, when the occupying British forces fled the city, they defiantly hoisted a Union Jack on a greased, uncleated flagpole so it couldn't be lowered; patriot John Van Arsdale drove his own cleats into the pole to replace the flag with the Stars and Stripes.

Continue around onto Water Street, passing on your right **New York Plaza,** a complex of high-tech office towers linked by an underground concourse. Just beyond it is the

6 **Vietnam Veterans Memorial,** where moving passages from the letters of servicemen and servicewomen have been etched into a wall of greenish glass set on a large brick plaza.

7 Return to Broad Street and go one block inland to **Fraunces Tavern,** a complex of five largely 19th-century buildings housing a museum, restaurant, and bar. The main building is a Colonial house (brick exterior, cream-colored marble portico and balcony) built in 1719 and converted to a tavern in 1762. This was also the site where, in 1783, George Washington delivered a farewell address to his officers celebrating the British evacuation from New York. Today Fraunces Tavern contains two fully furnished period rooms and other displays of 18th- and 19th-century American history. *54 Pearl St. at Broad St.,* ☎ *212/425–1778.* ☛ *$2.50 adults, $1 students, senior citizens. Museum open weekdays 10–4:45, Sat. noon–4.*

TIME OUT The brick plaza behind 85 Broad Street is flanked by a variety of small restaurants. Order a take-out meal or snack and eat it out here on the benches, where you can watch busy office workers milling past and enjoy not being one of them.

Head up Pearl Street to **Hanover Square,** a quiet tree-lined plaza that stood on the waterfront when the East River reached Pearl Street. This was the city's original printing-house square; on the site of 81 Pearl Street, William Bradford established the first printing press in the colonies. The pirate Captain Kidd lived in the neighborhood, and the graceful brownstone **India House** (1837) used to house the New York Cotton Exchange. Today it holds Harry's at Hanover Square, a vintage Wall Street bar.

Walk inland up Hanover Square to the rounded corner of South William and Beaver streets, where a graceful columned porch marks the entrance to **Delmonico's** restaurant, opened in 1888 on the site of an earlier Delmonico's founded in 1827. A pioneer in serving Continental cuisine, it was *the* place to go at the turn of the century; though now under different ownership, it is still a popular restaurant.

Two blocks farther north, William Street crosses **Wall Street,** so called because it traces the course of a wooden wall built across the island in 1653 to defend the Dutch colony against the native Indians. Arguably the most famous thoroughfare in the world, though only a third of a mile long, Wall Street began its financial career with stock traders conducting business along the sidewalks or at tables beneath a sheltering buttonwood tree. Today it's a dizzyingly narrow canyon—look to the right and you'll glimpse a sliver of East River waterfront; look to the left and you'll see the spire of Trinity Church, tightly framed by skyscrapers at the head of the street.

To learn the difference between Ionic and Corinthian columns, look at the **Citibank Building** to your right (55 Wall St.). The lower stories were part of an earlier U.S. Customs House, built in 1836–1842, and it was literally a bullish day on Wall Street when oxen hauled its 16 granite Ionic columns up to the site. When the National City Bank took over the building in 1899, they hired architects McKim, Mead & White to redesign the building, and in 1909 they added the second tier of columns but made them Corinthian.

One block west on Wall Street, where Broad Street becomes Nassau Street, you'll find on your right a regal statue of
❽ George Washington on the steps of the **Federal Hall National Memorial.** This 1883 statue by noted sculptor and presidential relative John Quincy Adams Ward marks the spot where Washington was sworn in as the first U.S. president in 1789. After the capital moved to Philadelphia in 1790, the origi-

nal Federal Hall became New York's City Hall, then was demolished in 1812 when the present City Hall was completed. The clean and simple lines of the current structure, built as (yet another) U.S. Customs House in 1842, were modeled after the Parthenon, a potent symbol for a young nation striving to emulate classical Greek democracy. It's now a museum featuring exhibits on New York and Wall Street. *26 Wall St.,* ☎ *212/264–8711.* ☛ *Free.* ☉ *Weekdays 9–5.*

In building a two-story investment bank at the corner of Wall and Broad streets, J. P. Morgan was in effect declaring himself above the pressures of Wall Street real-estate values. Now **Morgan Guaranty Trust,** the building bears pockmarks near the fourth window on the Wall Street side; these were created when a bomb that had been placed in a pushcart exploded in 1920.

⑨ Perhaps the heart of Wall Street is the **New York Stock Exchange,** which has its august Corinthian main entrance around the corner at 20 Broad Street. Compared with the Federal Hall memorial, this neoclassical building is much more elaborately decorated, as befitted the more grandiose national image of 1901, when it was designed. Inside, after what may be a lengthy wait, you can take an elevator to the third-floor visitor center. A self-guided tour, informative slide shows, video displays, and guides may help you interpret the seeming chaos you'll see from the visitors' gallery overlooking the immense (50-foot-high) trading hall. *Tickets available at 20 Broad St.,* ☎ *212/656–5165. Free tickets are distributed beginning at 9:05; come before 1 PM to assure getting in.* ☉ *Weekdays 9:15–4.*

⑩ **Trinity Church** (Broadway and Wall St.) was established as an Anglican parish in 1697. The present structure (1846), by Richard Upjohn, ranked as the city's tallest building for most of the second half of the 19th century. Its three huge bronze doors were designed by Richard Morris Hunt to recall Ghiberti's doors for the Baptistery in Florence, Italy. After the exterior sandstone was restored in 1991, New Yorkers were amazed to discover that a church they had always thought of as black was actually a rosy pink. The church's Gothic Revival interior is surprisingly light and elegant, although you may see derelicts napping in the pews. On the church's south side is a 2½-acre graveyard: Alexander Hamilton is buried beneath a white stone pyramid; and a monument commemorates Robert Fulton, the inventor of the steamboat (he's actually buried in the Livingstone family vault, with his wife).

⓫ Go back to Broadway and head north to **St. Paul's Chapel** (Broadway and Fulton St.), the oldest (1766) surviving church in Manhattan and the site of the prayer service following George Washington's inauguration as president. Built of rough Manhattan stone, it was modeled after London's St. Martin-in-the-Fields. It's open until 3 every day except Saturday for prayer and meditation; look in the north aisle for Washington's pew.

Walk down Fulton Street, named after the ferry to Brooklyn that once docked at its foot (the ferry itself was named after its inventor, Robert Fulton), to Water Street, which was once the shoreline. On the 19th-century landfill across ★ **⓬** the street is the 11-block **South Street Seaport Historic District,** which was created in 1967 to save this area from being overtaken by skyscrapers. The Rouse Corporation, which had already created slick so-called "festival marketplaces" in Boston (Quincy Market) and Baltimore (Harborplace), was hired to restore and adapt the existing historic buildings. Beyond it, Fulton Street, cobbled in blocks of Belgian granite, is a pedestrian mall that swarms with visitors, especially on fine-weather weekends. Immediately to your left is the **Cannon's Walk Block,** which contains 15 restored buildings.

At 211 Water Street is **Bowne & Co.,** a reconstructed working 19th-century print shop. Around the corner, a narrow court called Cannon's Walk, lined with shops, opens onto Fulton Street; follow it around to Front Street. Directly across Front Street is the **Fulton Market Building,** a modern building full of shops and restaurants, that re-creates the bustling commercial atmosphere of the old victual markets that occupied this site from 1822 on. On the south side of Fulton Street is the seaport's architectural centerpiece, **Schermerhorn Row,** a redbrick terrace of Georgian- and Federal-style warehouses and countinghouses built in 1811–12. Today the ground floors are occupied by upscale shops, bars, and restaurants, and the **South Street Seaport Museum.** *12 Fulton St.,* ☎ *212/669–9400.* ☛ *To ships, galleries, walking tours, Maritime Crafts Center, films, and other seaport events: $5 adults, $4 senior citizens, $3 students, $2 children.* ☉ *Daily 10–5.*

Cross South Street under an elevated stretch of the FDR Drive to **Pier 16,** where the historic ships are docked, including the *Peking,* the second-largest sailing ship in existence; the full-rigged *Wavertree;* and the lightship *Ambrose.* The Pier 16 ticket booth provides information and sells tickets to the museum, the ships, tours, and exhibits. Pier 16 is also the departure point for the one-hour **Seaport Liberty Cruise.** ☎ *212/630–8888. Fare: $12 adults, $10 senior citizens, $11 students, $6 children under 13. Runs late Mar.–Nov. Combination fares for cruise and other attractions: $15 adults, $14 senior citizens, $9 children.*

To the north is **Pier 17,** a multilevel dockside shopping mall. Its weathered-wood rear decks make a splendid spot from which to sit and contemplate the river; look north to see the Brooklyn, Manhattan, and Williamsburg bridges, and look across to see Brooklyn Heights.

Return along Fulton Street to Broadway and walk two blocks north to the so-called Cathedral of Commerce, the ❸ ornate white terra-cotta **Woolworth Building** (Park Pl. and Broadway). When it opened in 1913 it was, at 792 feet, the world's tallest building; it still houses the Woolworth corporate offices. Take a peek at the lobby: Among its extravagant Gothic-style details are sculptures set into arches in the lobby ceiling; one of them represents an elderly F. W. Woolworth pinching his pennies, while another depicts the architect, Cass Gilbert, cradling in his arms a model of his creation.

Across Broadway is triangular **City Hall Park,** originally the town common. A bronze statue of patriot Nathan Hale, who was hanged as a spy by the British troops occupying New York City, stands on the Broadway side of the park. In its day this green spot has hosted hangings, riots, and demonstrations; it is also the finish line for ticker-tape parades up lower Broadway (though ticker-tape is nowadays

replaced with perforated margin strips torn off from trac-
tor-feed computer paper).

⓮   **City Hall,** built between 1803 and 1812, is unexpectedly se-
date, small-scale, and charming. Its exterior columns reflect
the classical influence of Greece and Rome, and the handsome cast-iron cupola is crowned with a statue of Lady Justice. Originally its front and sides were clad in white marble
while the back was faced in cheap brownstone, because the
city fathers assumed New York would never grow farther
north than this. (Limestone now covers all four sides.) The
major interior feature is a domed rotunda from which a
sweeping marble double staircase leads to the second-floor
public rooms. The Victorian-style City Council Chamber
in the east wing is small and clubby, with mahogany detailing and ornate gilding; the Board of Estimate chamber
to the west has colonial paintings and church-pew-style seating; and the Governor's Room at the head of the stairs, used
for ceremonial events, is filled with historic portraits and
furniture, including a writing table George Washington
used in 1789 when New York was the U.S. capital. ☏
212/788–6879 for tour info.

Just south of the Municipal Building, a ramp curves up into
★ **⓯**   the pedestrian walkway over the **Brooklyn Bridge.** The
Great Bridge promenade takes a half-hour to walk and is
a New York experience on a par with the Statue of Liberty
trip or the Empire State Building ascent; you don't need
binoculars to enjoy the vistas, but you'd do well to bring
a hat or scarf, because the wind whips through the cables
like a dervish. Before this bridge was built, Brooklynites had
to rely on the Fulton Street ferry to get to Brooklyn—a
charming way to travel, surely, but unreliable in the fog and
ice of winter. After some 50 years of talk about a bridge,
John Augustus Roebling, a respected engineer, was handed
a bridge construction assignment in 1867. As the project
to build the first steel suspension bridge slowly took shape
over the next 15 years, it captured the imagination of the
city; on its completion in 1883, it was called the Eighth Wonder of the World. Its twin Gothic-arched towers rise 268
feet from the river below. The roadway is supported by a
web of steel cables, hung from the towers and attached to
block-long anchorages on either shore. It is hardly the

longest suspension bridge in the world anymore, but it remains a symbol of what humans can accomplish.

★ ⑯ Backtrack across Broadway and turn down Church Street to the **World Trade Center,** a 16-acre, 12-million-square-foot complex that contains New York's two tallest buildings (1,350 feet high). To reach the observation deck on the 107th floor of 2 World Trade Center, elevators glide a quarter of a mile into the sky—in only 58 seconds. The view potentially extends 55 miles, although signs at the ticket window disclose how far you can see that day and whether the outdoor deck is open. In February 1993, the Center was the site of a bombing, attributed to terrorists, that killed six people and caused extensive damage to the area. However, the Center has, for the most part, returned to normal operations, though security has been tightened considerably within the complex. From December 1995, you should once again be able to get the same view with a meal at **Windows on the World** (☎ 212/938–1100) atop 1 World Trade Center—a New York favorite that has been sorely missed during its long closure (jacket required). ☎ *212/435–7377.* ☞ *$4.75 adults, $2.25 senior citizens, $2.50 children.* ☉ *June–Sept., daily 9:30 AM–11:30 PM; Oct.–May, daily 9:30 AM–9:30 PM.*

Some 50,000 people work in this seven-building complex, and at street level and underground it contains more than 60 stores, services, and restaurants. There's a TKTS booth selling discount tickets to Broadway and Off-Broadway shows in the mezzanine of 2 World Trade Center (open weekdays 11–5:30, Sat. 11–1), and on the ninth floor of 4 World Trade Center, a visitors' gallery overlooks the trading floor of the Commodities Exchange (☎ 212/938–2025; open weekdays 9:30–3).

More than a million cubic yards of rock and soil were excavated for the World Trade Center—and then moved across West Street to help beget the 100-acre Battery Park City development, a complete neighborhood built from scratch. Take the pedestrian overpass north of 1 World Trade ⑰ Center to Battery Park City's centerpiece, the **World Financial Center** (☎ 212/945–0505), a four-tower complex designed by Cesar Pelli, with some heavy-duty corporate tenants, in-

cluding Merrill Lynch, American Express, and Dow Jones.
You'll come out into the soaring **Winter Garden Atrium,** its
mauve marble cascade of steps spilling down into a vaulted
plaza with 16 giant palm trees, framed by a vast arched window overlooking the Hudson. Surrounding the atrium are
several upscale shops—Godiva chocolatiers, Rizzoli bookstore, Platypus for unusual housewares, Barneys NY for
menswear—plus a skylit food court.

Of the few spots in Manhattan that directly overlook the
rivers, **Battery Park City** just may be the best. The outdoor
plaza right behind the atrium curls around a tidy little
yacht basin; take in the view of the Statue of Liberty and
read the stirring quotations worked into the iron railings.
Just north of the basin is the terminal for ferry service to
Hoboken, New Jersey (☎ 908/463–3779; fare: $2), on the
other side of the Hudson River. It's an eight-minute ride to
Frank Sinatra's hometown, with a spectacular view of
lower Manhattan. Beyond the ferry terminal is the southern end of the new **Hudson River Park,** a landscaped park
with playgrounds, promenades and walkways, handball and
basketball courts, and grassy areas strewn with downtown
residents soaking up rays on sunny days.

To the south, a longer riverside promenade that eventually
will connect with Battery Park accompanies the residential
part of Battery Park City, a mix of high rises, town houses,
shops, and green squares that does a surprisingly good job
of duplicating the rhythms of the rest of the city. Especially
noteworthy among the art works populating the esplanade
are Ned Smyth's columned plaza with chessboards; and the
South Cove, a collaborative effort, a romantic curved stage
set of wood piers and a steel-frame lookout.

Off the Beaten Track

The Cloisters. Perched atop a wooded hilltop near Manhattan's northernmost tip, the Cloisters houses the
Metropolitan Museum of Art's medieval collection in the
style of a medieval monastery. Colonnaded walks connect
authentic French and Spanish monastic cloisters, a French
Romanesque chapel, a 12th-century chapter house, and a
Romanesque apse. An entire room is devoted to a superb

set of 15th- and 16th-century tapestries depicting a unicorn hunt. The view of the Hudson River and the New Jersey Palisades (an undeveloped Rockefeller family preserve) enhances the experience. The M–4 "Cloisters–Fort Tryon Park" bus provides a lengthy but scenic ride; catch it along Madison Avenue below 110th Street, or Broadway above; or take the A subway to 190th Street. *Fort Tryon Park,* ☎ *212/923–3700. Suggested contribution: $7 adults, $3.50 senior citizens and students.* ☉ *Tues.–Sun. 9:30–5:15; Nov.–Feb. closes at 4:45.*

The **Brooklyn Botanic Garden** occupies 52 acres across Flatbush Avenue from Prospect Park. The garden exudes a beguiling Oriental atmosphere, due to the presence of a **Japanese Garden,** complete with a blazing red torii gate and a pond laid out in the shape of the Chinese character for "heart." Wander through the **Cranford Rose Garden** (5,000 bushes, 1,200 varieties); the **Fragrance Garden,** designed especially for the blind; and the **Shakespeare Garden,** featuring 80 plants immortalized by the bard (including roses of many names). A complex of handsome greenhouses called the **Steinhardt Conservatory** holds thriving desert, tropical, temperate, and aquatic vegetation, as well as a display charting the evolution of plants over the past 140 million years. *1000 Washington Ave. near Empire Blvd.,* ☎ *718/622–4433.* ☛ *To grounds free.* ☉ *Apr.–Sept. Tues.–Fri. 8–6, weekends and holidays 10–6; Oct.–Mar. Tues.–Fri. 8–4:30, weekends and holidays 10–4:30.* ☛ *To Steinhardt Conservatory Nov.–Mar. free; Apr.–Oct., $2 adults, $1 senior citizens and children 3–12.* ☉ *Apr.–Sept., Tues.–Sun. 10–5; Oct.–Mar., Tues.–Sun. 10–4.*

The **Brooklyn Museum,** housed in a stunningly regal building designed by the McKim, Mead & White team in 1897, sports huge statues of Brooklyn and Manhattan (as classical ladies) on its Eastern Parkway front. With approximately 1.5 million objects, the Brooklyn collection is the seventh largest in the country. The museum's renovation and expansion project by Japanese architect Arata Isozaki and New York firm James Stewart Polshek includes a new auditorium with a wavelike ceiling, and new galleries in the oldest part of the building, adding 30,000 square feet of exhibition space. Look especially for its **Egyptian Art** collection (third floor), considered the best of its kind anywhere outside London or Cairo, or the **African and Pre-Columbian Art** (first floor), another collection recognized worldwide. The museum also offers excellent special exhibitions, a treasure chest of a gift shop, and dramatic views of Manhattan from its Eastern Parkway–Washington Avenue corner. *200 Eastern Pkwy.,* ☎ *718/638–5000. Suggested contribution: $4 adults, $1.50 senior citizens, $2 students.* ◎ *Wed.–Sun. 10–5.*

The **Bronx Zoo,** recently renamed the **International Wildlife Conservation Park,** is the nation's largest urban zoo (265 acres). It deserves nearly an entire day's visit on its own; if you want to return on another day, you can take the Liberty Lines BxM11 bus that runs up Madison Avenue (☎ 718/652–8400; fare: $4). At the zoo you'll see two different historical methods of keeping wild animals. The turn-of-the-century zoological garden houses monkeys, sea lions, and elephants (among many others) in fancy Beaux Arts–style edifices at **Astor Court.** It's being gradually replaced by the animal-in-habitat approach used in the **World of Birds,** with its capacious walk-through indoor natural habitats; in **Jungleworld,** an indoor tropical rain forest complete with five waterfalls, millipedes, flowering orchids, and pythons; and in **Baboon Reserve,** with dry riverbeds and a simulated archeological dig. The **Children's Zoo** (☛ $1.50; open Apr.–Oct.) features many hands-on learning activities, as well as a large petting zoo. At the **Zoo Center,** visitors will find a rare Sumatran rhino. The zoo as a whole has more than 4,000 animals representing 667 species. *Bronx Zoo,* ☎ *718/367–1010.* ☛ *Thurs.–Tues. $5.75 adults, $2 senior citizens and children 2–12 (Nov.–Feb. $2.50 adults, $1 senior citizens and children); free Wed.* ◎ *Feb.–Oct., weekdays 10–5, weekends and holidays 10–5:30; Nov.–Jan., daily 10–4:30.*

What to See and Do with Children

New York is as magical a place for children as it is for adults. For calendars of children's events, consult New York magazine and the weekly *Village Voice* newspaper, available at newsstands. The Friday *New York Times* "Weekend" section provides a good listing of children's activities.

Sightseeing

As far as outdoor sights are concerned, there is plenty to please; surprising pockets of street sculpture, graffiti art, strange building facades, and quirky shop windows may be found on almost every block. In no other city are you more likely to entertain offspring simply by wandering. Children get a kick from the sheer size of the buildings, and from riding cabs, or even buses and subways (especially the first or last car, with a view of the track and tunnels). For more exotic transportation, try the **horse-drawn carriages** around Central Park (at Grand Army Plaza or intersections of Central Park S, between 5th and 7th Aves.; $34 for the first 20 minutes); a 19th-century schooner, named *The Pioneer* (South St. Seaport, ☎ 212/748–8784; $16 adults, $13 children under 12, for 2 hours); hydroliners named *Express I and II* (Pier 11, two blocks south of the South Street Seaport, ☎ 800/262-8743; $15 adults, $8 children under 12, for 75 minutes); or an **Island Helicopter** tour (34th St. and East River, ☎ 212/683–4575; $47–$119). For little more than the price of a subway token, the **Roosevelt Island Aerial Tramway** across the East River is a sure hit. Trams board at 2nd Avenue and 60th Street and run every 15 minutes during regular hours, and every 7½ minutes during rush hours, which you might wish to avoid.

Museums

Although just about every major museum in New York City has something to interest children, certain ones hold special appeal. At the top of the list is the **American Museum of Natural History** (Central Park West, at W. 79th St., ☎ 212/769–5100), with its lifelike dioramas and newly restored collection of giant dinosaurs, including a huge Tyrannosaurus rex. Also intriguing are the Discovery Room, with hands-on exhibits for children, and the Naturemax Theater, which shows awesome nature films on a gigantic screen. The adjacent **Hayden Planetarium** offers astronomical exhibits and sky shows; there is also a preschool show (reservations required; ☎ 212/769–5920) (*see* Tour 8, *above*).

The **Children's Museum of Manhattan** is a kind of indoor playground for kids 2–12, with interactive exhibits organized around common childhood experiences. Children can climb, crawl, paint, make collages, and try on costumes.

212 W. 83rd St., ☏ 212/721–1234. ☛ $5 adults and children, $2.50 senior citizens. ⊘ Mon., Wed., and Thurs. 1:30–5:30, Fri.–Sun. 10–5.

The **Children's Museum of the Arts,** in a loftlike space in SoHo, allows children ages 1 to 10 to become actively involved in visual and performing arts. Highlights include the Monet Ball Pond, where children can play with brightly colored balls near a water-lily mural; the Lines and Shapes alcove, where kids have access to computer drawing; and the Creative Play area, which provides a large playpen, a reading corner, art activities, and cushions and futons for relaxation. Weekend workshops are included in the ☛ price, plus a $1 materials fee. *72 Spring St., ☏ 212/941–9198. ☛ Weekdays $4 and weekends $5 for adults under 65 and children over 18 months. ⊘ Tues.–Sun. 11–5.*

Another favorite with the younger generation is the **Intrepid Sea-Air-Space Museum,** an immense World War II aircraft carrier. On deck is a startling array of aircraft; inside there are aviation and military exhibits, as well as skinny hallways, winding staircases, and dozens of knobs, buttons, and wheels to manipulate. *Pier 86 at 12th Ave. and W. 46th St., ☏ 212/245–0072. ☛ $7 adults, $6 senior citizens and veterans, $4 children 6–11. ⊘ Wed.–Sun. 10–5.*

Another good bet is the **New York City Fire Museum** (278 Spring St., ☏ 212/691–1303), with displays of fire-fighting equipment and tours given by real firefighters.

The **Brooklyn Museum** has special programs for kids and families. For children who like hands-on involvement, the place to go is the **Brooklyn Children's Museum,** considered one of the best in the world, and full of tunnels, bubbles, animals, and neon lights. Exhibits cover the environment, nature, science, and more. *145 Brooklyn Ave., ☏ 718/735–4432. Suggested contribution: $3. ⊘ June–Aug., Mon. and Wed.–Sun. noon–5; Sept.–May, Wed.–Fri. 2–5, weekends and holidays noon–5.*

The Arts and Entertainment

Madison Square Garden (7th Ave., between 31st and 33rd Sts., ☏ 212/465–6000) offers, besides sports events, some Disney and *Sesame Street* extravaganzas that appeal especially to children. There are major ice shows in winter, and each spring brings the **Ringling Bros. Barnum & Bailey Circus** (check local newspapers for dates, times, and ticket information). Meanwhile, the **Big Apple Circus** (35 W. 35th St., ☎ 212/268–0055) charms the toughest New Yorkers in locations all over the five boroughs during spring and summer and in residence at Lincoln Center from October through January.

Little People's Theater (The Courtyard Playhouse, 39 Grove St., between W. 4th St. and 7th Ave., ☎ 212/765–9540) brings fairy tales and nursery rhymes to life on Sunday afternoons. **New York Children's Theater** (Lincoln Sq. Theater, 250 W. 65th St., ☎ 212/496–8009) is determinedly realistic in style and explores topics such as literacy and aging. The **International Festival of Puppet Theater,** sponsored by the Jim Henson Foundation, takes place in the summer at the Joseph Papp Public Theater (425 Lafayette St., ☎ 212/598–7107); **Marionette Theater** (Swedish Cottage, Central Park at W. 81st St., ☎ 212/988–9093) features programs Tuesday–Saturday.

3 Shopping

SHOPPING IN NEW YORK IS THEATER, architecture, and people-watching all rolled into one. Big stores and small ones, one-of-a-kinds and chains together present an overwhelming array of "Things." Another big Manhattan shopping lure is the bargain. Major intersections are instant markets as street peddlers hawk fake Gucci and Cartier watches at $15–$25 each. (These may just possibly last a year or two.) There are thrift shops and resale shops where well-known socialites send their castoffs and Catherine Deneuve snaps up antique lace. At off-price and discount stores, markdowns result in substantial savings, and the sales are even better. Designers' showroom sales allow you to buy cheap at the source; auctions promise good prices as well.

By Karen
Cure

Updated
by Dick
Kagan

Stores are generally open Monday–Saturday from 10 AM to 5 or 6 PM, but neighborhood peculiarities do exist. Most stores on the Lower East Side and in the diamond district on 47th Street close on Friday afternoon and all day Saturday for the Jewish Sabbath while keeping normal hours on Sunday. Sunday hours, also common on the West Side and in Greenwich Village and SoHo, are the exception on the Upper East Side.

Shopping Neighborhoods

South Street Seaport
The Seaport's shops are located along the cobbled, pedestrians-only extension to Fulton Street; in the Fulton Market building, the original home of the city's fish market; and on the three levels of Pier 17. You'll find many outstanding retailers: **Laura Ashley** for women's clothing, **Brookstone** for gadgets and hardware, **Caswell-Massey** for fragrances, and **Sharper Image** for high-tech gimmickry. The big catalog house **J. Crew** chose the Seaport as the location for its first retail outlet. There are also few-of-a-kind shops, notably **Bowne & Co.,** an old-fashioned print shop.

World Financial Center
Although the nearby World Trade Center bills its concourse as the city's busiest shopping center, the World Fi-

No matter where you go, travel is easier when you know the code.^{SM}

dial 1 8 0 0
C A L L
A T T®

Dial 1 800 CALL ATT and you'll always get through from any phone with any card* and you'll always get AT&T's best deal.** It's the one number ~~~~member when calling

575 Fifth
Avenue, **9**

Barney's New
York, **13, 2**

Bergdorf
Goodman, **3**

Bloomingdale's **1**

Century 21, **18**

Henri Bendel, **4**

Herald
Center, **12**

Lord &
Taylor, **10**

Lower East Side
(Orchard
Street), **14**

Macy's, **11**

Manhattan Art
and Antiques
Center, **6**

Rockefeller
Center, **7**

Saks Fifth
Avenue, **8**

South Street
Seaport, **17**

Trump Tower, **5**

World Financial
Center, **15**

World Trade
Center, **16**

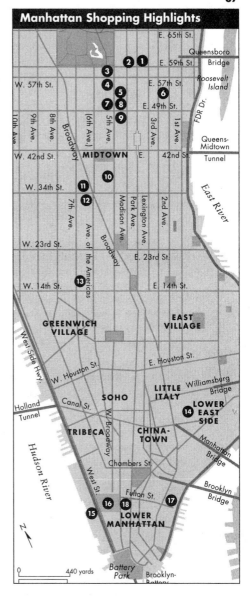

Manhattan Shopping Highlights

nancial Center in Battery Park City is a shopping destination to reckon with, thanks to stores such as **Godiva Chocolatier** for chocolates and **Offermann** for leather goods. **Quest Toys** has a wonderful selection of wooden and educational playthings. Most are open on Sundays.

Lower East Side

Once home to millions of Jewish immigrants from Russia and Eastern Europe, this area is New Yorkers' bargain beat. The center of it all is narrow, unprepossessing Orchard Street, which is crammed with tiny, no-nonsense clothing and shoe stores ranging from kitschy to elegant. Start at Houston Street, walk down one side as far as Canal Street, then walk back up. Essential stops include **Fine & Klein** for handbags; **Forman's** for women's clothing; and **Lace-Up Shoes.**

SoHo

On West Broadway, SoHo's main drag, and on Broadway and Wooster, Greene, Mercer, Prince, Spring, Broome, and Grand streets, major art galleries keep company with chic clothing stores such as **Yohji Yamamoto** and **Agnès B.** Well-known stops include decorative-items specialist **Wolfman-Gold & Good Company** and Southwest- and Italian-themed **Zona.** Many stores in SoHo are open seven days a week.

Lower 5th Avenue

Fifth Avenue south of 23rd Street along with the streets fanning east and west are home to some of New York's hippest shops and a lively downtown crowd. Many of the locals sport clothes from the neighborhood—a mix of the hip like **Emporio Armani, Paul Smith,** and **Matsuda** (for Japanese clothing) as well as discount clothiers such as **BFO** and **Moe Ginsburg.** A block away in the same latitudes on 6th Avenue is a cluster of superstores, including a gargantuan **Barnes & Noble** and a colossal **Bed, Bath & Beyond. Barneys, Williams-Sonoma,** and **Pottery Barn** are within walking distance on nearby 7th Avenue.

Herald Square

Reasonable prices prevail at this intersection of 34th Street and Avenue of the Americas (6th Avenue). Giant **Macy's** has traditionally been the linchpin. Opposite is Manhattan's first **Toys "R" Us.** Next door on 6th Avenue, the seven-story Manhattan Mall is anchored by **Stern's** department store, which makes for wonderful browsing.

Midtown Near Grand Central

Some of the best-known men's clothiers are here on and just off the stretch of Madison Avenue nicknamed Trad Avenue: **J. Press, Brooks Brothers, Paul Stuart, Chipp** custom tailors, **Jos. A Bank,** and **Wallachs.** Most also handle women's clothing in dress-for-success styles.

5th Avenue

The boulevard that was once home to some of the biggest names in New York retailing is not what it once was, that role having been usurped by Madison Avenue north of 57th Street. But 5th Avenue from Central Park South to Rockefeller Center still shines with **F.A.O. Schwarz** and **Bergdorf Goodman** (both the main store and **Bergdorf Goodman Men** are at 58th St.), **Tiffany** and **Bulgari** jewelers (at 57th St.), **Takashimaya** (at 54th St.), **Cartier** jewelers (at 52nd St.), and so on down to **Saks Fifth Avenue** (at 50th St.). **Rockefeller Center** itself provides a plethora of shops. To the south (at 47th St.) is the shiny 575 atrium mall, named for its 5th Avenue address, and the venerable **Lord & Taylor** department store (at 39th St.).

Columbus Avenue

Between 66th and 86th streets, this former tenement district is now home to some of the city's glitziest stores. Shops are mostly modern in design, upscale but not top-of-the-line. Clothing runs the gamut from traditional for men and women (**Frank Stella Ltd.**) to high funk (**Betsey Johnson**) and high style (**Charivari**).

Upper East Side

On Madison and Lexington avenues, roughly between 57th and 79th streets, New York branches of world-renowned designer boutiques are joined by spirited retailers who fill their stores with the unique and stylish. Domestic and imported items for the home, fine antiques, and wonderful clothing predominate—and the prices aren't always sky high.

Department Stores

ABC Carpet & Home (888 and 881 Broadway, at 19th St., ☎ 212/473–3000). This huge emporium has just about everything for the home, from antique armoires to modern, state-of-the-art TVs and stereos, from every imaginable bath and bedroom accessory to baby gifts and dinnerware. Then there are the floor coverings: they range from the most exotic Orientals to basic vinyl tiles. It's easy to while away an entire afternoon here.

Barneys New York (106 7th Ave., at 17th St., ☎ 212/929–9000; Madison Ave. at 61st St., ☎ 212/826–8900; World Financial Center, ☎ 212/945–1600). Founded as a menswear discounter some 60 years ago, Barneys is still the place to see what's hot. The still-extensive selection of menswear ranges from made-to-measure and European and American designer labels to mass-market natural-shouldered suits; the women's department is a showcase of current women's fashion. The ladies' accessories are some of the chicest around, and the Chelsea Passage can be counted on for distinctive housewares and gifts.

Bergdorf Goodman (754 5th Ave., between 57th and 58th Sts., ☎ 212/753–7300). Good taste reigns in an elegant and understated setting. The Home Department is room after exquisite room of wonderful linens, tabletop items, and gifts. The expanded men's store, across the street, occupies the former home of the giant F.A.O. Schwarz toy store (now at 767 5th Ave.).

Bloomingdale's (1000 3rd Ave., at 59th St., ☎ 212/355–5900). Only a handful of department stores occupy an entire city block; Macy's is one, and this New York institution is another. The main floor is a stupefying maze of cosmetic counters, mirrors, and black walls; elsewhere the racks are overfull, salespeople overworked, and the departments constantly on the move. Still, selections are dazzling at all but the lowest price points, and the markdowns on top-of-the-line designer goods can be extremely rewarding.

Henri Bendel (712 5th Ave., between 55th and 56th Sts., ☎ 212/247–1100). Now firmly established under its beautiful new roof (having moved from W. 57th Street), Bendel's continues to delight with its stylish displays and sophisticated boutiques. The second-floor café is a delight.

Lord & Taylor (424 5th Ave., between 38th and 39th Sts., ☎ 212/391–3344). This store can be relied upon for the wearable, the fashionable, and the classic in clothes and accessories for women. It's refined, well stocked, and never overwhelming.

Macy's (Herald Sq., Broadway at 34th St., ☎ 212/695–4400). No less than a miracle on 34th Street, Macy's main store is the largest retail store in America. Over the past two decades, it has grown chic and much more au courant in the style department, but its main floor is reassuringly traditional. The latest trends are represented in almost every area the store covers. Estate Jewelry offers fine antique pieces. And for cooking gear and housewares, the Cellar nearly outdoes Zabar's.

Saks Fifth Avenue (611 5th Ave., between 49th and 50th Sts., ☎ 212/753–4000). This wonderful store still embodies the spirit of service and style with which it opened in 1926. Saks believes in good manners, the ceremonies of life, and dressing for the part; the selection for men, women, and children—doubled by recent expansion—affirms this quality.

Takashimaya New York (693 5th Ave., between 54th and 55th Sts., ☎ 212/350–0100). This pristine branch of Japan's largest department store carries stylish clothes for women and men and fine household items, all of which reflect a combination of Eastern and Western designs. The garden atrium and two-floor art gallery contribute to the elegant ambience.

Specialty Shops

Antiques

Manhattan Art & Antiques Center (1050 2nd Ave., between 55th and 56th Sts., ☎ 212/355–4400). More than 100 dealers stocking everything from paisley and Judaica to satsuma, scientifica, and samovars jumble the three floors here. The level of quality is not, as a rule, up to that of Madison Avenue, but then neither are the prices.

Metropolitan Arts and Antiques Pavilion (110 W. 19th St., between 6th Ave. and 7th Ave., ☎ 212/463–0200). Good for costume jewelry, off-beat bric-a-brac, and '50s kitsch, this antiques mall holds regularly scheduled auctions and specialty shows featuring rare books, photography, tribal art, Victoriana, and other lots.

Art Galleries

Gagosian (980 Madison Ave., between 76th and 77th Sts., ☎ 212/744–2313; 136 Wooster St., ☎ 212/228–2828). Works on display are by such artists as Richard Serra, Willem De Kooning, Jasper Johns, Frank Stella, Warhol, David Salle, and Philip Taaffe.

Hirschl & Adler (21 E. 70th St., ☎ 212/535–8810). A respected dealer of American painting and sculpture, this gallery also offers American decorative arts. Among the celebrated artists whose works are featured: Thomas Cole, Childe Hassam, Ralston Crawford, John Storrs, and William Merritt Chase.

Books

Gotham Book Mart (41 W. 47th St., ☎ 212/719–4448). The late Frances Steloff opened this store years ago with just $200 in her pocket, half of it on loan. But she helped launch *Ulysses*, D. H. Lawrence, and Henry Miller and is now legendary among bibliophiles, as is her bookstore, an oasis for those who love to read, with nearly a quarter of a million books.

Rizzoli (31 W. 57th St., ☎ 212/759–2424; 454 W. Broadway, ☎ 212/674–1616; World Financial Center, ☎ 212/385–1400). Uptown, an elegant marble entrance, oak paneling, chandeliers, and classical music accompany books and magazines on art, architecture, dance, design, foreign language, and travel; the downtown stores come with fewer frills.

Strand (828 Broadway, at 12th St., ☎ 212/473–1452). Eight miles of shelves house more than 2 million books at this biggest of Manhattan's used-book stores.

Cameras and Electronics

47th Street Photo (67 W. 47th St., 115 W. 45th St.; ☎ 212/921–1287). Prices can be better elsewhere, but these stores manned by Hasidic Jews are a heavyweight among electronics discounters. Note Friday afternoon and Saturday closings.

CDs, Tapes, and Records

Tower Records (692 Broadway, at 4th St., ☎ 212/505–1500; 1961 Broadway, at 66th St., ☎ 212/799–2500; 1535 3rd

Ave., at 87th St., ☎ 212/369–2500; 725 5th Ave., basement level of Trump Tower, 212/838–8110). The selection of CDs and tapes can get overwhelming here: The scene is pure New York.

Children's Clothing

Cerutti (807 Madison Ave., between 67th and 68th Sts., ☎ 212/737–7540). This is where Nanny takes her Little Princess and Yoko Ono shopped for Sean Lennon when he was a tyke.

Crystal

Three peerless sources are **Baccarat** (625 Madison Ave., between 58th and 59th Sts., ☎ 212/826–4100); **Hoya Crystal Gallery** (450 Park Ave., between 56th and 57th Sts., ☎ 212/223–6335); and **Steuben** (717 5th Ave., at 56th St., ☎ 212/752–1441). **Rogaška** (685 Madison Ave., between 61st and 62nd Sts.) is a newcomer offering understated classic wares made in Slovenia at relatively modest prices.

Food

Balducci's (424 6th Ave., at 9th St., ☎ 212/673–2600). In this former mom-and-pop food shop, now one of the city's finest food stores, mounds of baby carrots keep company with frilly lettuce, feathery dill, and superlative meats, fish, cheeses, chocolates, baked goods, pastas, vinegars, oils, and Italian specialties.

Kam-Man (200 Canal St., ☎ 212/571–0330). The city's premier Chinese market, Kam-Man is filled with exotic foods, the staccato sound of Chinese, and mysterious smells.

Zabar's (2245 Broadway, at 80th St., ☎ 212/787–2000). Enjoy the atmosphere of one of New York's favorite food markets. Dried herbs and spices, chocolates, and assorted bottled foods are downstairs, along with a fragrant jumble of fresh breads and the cheese, meat, and smoked-fish counters. Upstairs is one of New York's largest selections of kitchenware.

Fragrance Shops

Aveda Aromatherapy Esthetique (509 Madison Ave., between 52nd and 53rd Sts., ☎ 212/832–2416; 456 W. Broadway, between Prince and Houston Sts., ☎ 212/473–0280). Concoct your own perfumes from the impressive selection of essential oils.

Floris (703 Madison Ave., between 62nd and 63rd Sts., ☎ 212/935–9100). Floral English toiletries beloved of such beauties as Cher, Sophia Loren, and Catherine Deneuve fill this re-creation of the cozy London original.

Home Decor and Gifts

Charlotte Moss & Co. (1027 Lexington Ave., between 73rd and 74th Sts., ☎ 212/772–3320). Within what looks like a vine-wrapped, chintz-cozy English country house, you'll find charming pieces, such as a replica of Lady Nancy Astor's button-tufted slipper chair.

Felissimo (10 W. 56th St., ☎ 212/247–5656). Spread over four stories of a Beaux Arts townhouse are unusual items, many handcrafted either in the U.S. or abroad, which reconcile classic European and modern Asian sensibilities. The goods include vases, candlesticks, garden utensils, and even bird cages, as well as linens and bath accessories.

Jewelry, Watches, and Silver

Fortunoff (681 5th Ave., between 53rd and 54th Sts., ☎ 212/758–6660). Good prices on gold and silver jewelry, flatware, and hollow-ware draw crowds to this large store.

James Robinson (480 Park Ave., at 58th St., ☎ 212/752–6166). This family-owned business sells handmade flatware, antique silver, fine estate jewelry, and 18th- and 19th-century china.

Tiffany & Co. (727 5th Ave., at 57th St., ☎ 212/755–8000). A shiny robin's-egg-blue box from this venerable New York jeweler announces the contents as something very special. Along with the $80,000 platinum-and-diamond bracelets, there is a great deal that's affordable on a whim.

Luggage and Leather Goods

Crouch & Fitzgerald (400 Madison Ave., at 48th St., ☎ 212/755–5888). Since 1839, this store has offered a terrific selection in hard- and soft-sided luggage, plus handbags.

T. Anthony (445 Park Ave., at 56th St., ☎ 212/750–9797). This store's hard-and soft-sided luggage of coated fabric with leather trim has brass fasteners that look like precision machines.

Menswear

Brooks Brothers (346 Madison Ave., at 44th St., ☎ 212/682–8800). An American-menswear institution, with conservative styles in both suits and sportswear.

Façonnable (689 5th Ave., at 54th St., ☎ 212/319–0111). Designed in France, the well-made traditional clothing and sportswear has an international appeal.

Paul Smith (108 5th Ave., at 16th St., ☎ 212/627–9770). Dark mahogany Victorian cases display downtown styles.

Paul Stuart (Madison Ave., at 45th St., ☎ 212/682–0320). The fabric selection is interesting, the tailoring superb, and the look traditional but not stodgy.

Saint Laurie, Ltd. (897 Broadway, between 19th and 20th Sts., ☎ 212/473–0100). This family-owned business sells suits manufactured on the premises in styles ranging from boxy traditional to the Italianate in lovely fabrics.

MEN'S SHOES

Church's English Shoes (428 Madison Ave., at 49th St., ☎ 212/755–4313). This store has been selling beautifully made English shoes since 1873.

Tootsie Plohound (137 5th Ave., at 20th St., ☎ 212/460–8650; 413 W. Broadway, between Prince and Spring Sts., ☎ 212/925–8931). These shops are tops for "downtown" shoes: fun, funky, and cool. They carry women's styles, too.

Paper, Greeting Cards, Stationery

Kate's Paperie (561 Broadway, at Prince St., ☎ 212/941–9816; 8 W. 13th St., ☎ 212/633–0570). These wonderful spots feature fabulous wrapping papers, some handmade; bound blank books; and more.

Toys

F.A.O. Schwarz (767 5th Ave., at 58th St., ☎ 212/644–9400). You will be hooked on this sprawling two-level children's store from the minute you walk through the door and one of the costumed staff members—a donkey, a clown, a cave woman, or a mad scientist—extends a welcome.

Women's Clothing

CLASSICISTS

Ann Taylor (2017 Broadway, near 69th St., ☎ 212/873–7344; 25 Fulton St., ☎ 212/608–5600; 805 3rd Ave., at 50th St., ☎ 212/308–5333; 3 E. 57th St., ☎ 212/832–2010;

and other locations). These stores provide what the elegant young woman with a sense of style needs for work and play.

DESIGNER SHOWCASES

Chanel (5 E. 57th St., ☎ 212/355–5050). The classic designs here never go out of style; neither do those wonderful Chanel perfumes.

Comme des Garçons (116 Wooster St., ☎ 212/219–0660). This SoHo shop showcases Japanese designer Rei Kawakubo.

Emporio Armani (110 5th Ave., between 16th and 17th Sts., ☎ 212/727–3240). The Italian designer's casual line is featured.

Gianni Versace (817 Madison Ave., between 68th and 69th Sts., ☎ 212/744–6868). An Italian maestro of color and form continues to dazzle with his daring.

Giorgio Armani (815 Madison Ave., between 68th and 69th Sts., ☎ 212/988–9191). In this lofty blond-and-beige space with grand, arched windows and doors, Armani's high-end line looks oh-so-chic.

Hermès (11 E. 57th St., ☎ 212/751–3181). Patterned silk scarves and the so-called "Kelly" handbags are hallmarks.

Polo/Ralph Lauren (867 Madison Ave., at 72nd St., ☎ 212/606–2100). Lauren's flagship store is one of New York's most distinctive shopping experiences, in a grand, carefully renovated turn-of-the-century town house. The new Polo Sport is directly across the street.

Valentino (823 Madison Ave., between 68th and 69th Sts., ☎ 212/744–0200). The mix here is at once audacious and beautifully cut, with the best of France and Italy on its racks.

Vera Wang (991 Madison Ave., at 77th St., ☎ 212/628–3400). Sumptuous, made-to-order bridal and evening wear is shown here by appointment only. Their periodic prêt-à-porter sales offer designer dresses for a (relative) song.

Yohji Yamamoto (103 Grand St., ☎ 212/966–9066). Severe, beautifully cut fashions come from fashion's Zen master.

DISCOUNT

Century 21 (22 Cortlandt St., between Broadway and Church St., ☎ 212/227–9092; 472 86th St., Bay Ridge, Brooklyn, ☎ 718/748–3266). Spiffy quarters make bargain-hunting a pleasure, and there are fabulous buys on very high fashion. Note that there are no try-ons, but items may be returned within 12 working days after purchase.

HIP STYLES

Reminiscence (74 5th Ave., between 13th and 14th Sts., ☎ 212/243–2292). The theme is strictly '50s and '60s, in vintage and new clothing.

Trash and Vaudeville (4 St. Marks Pl., ☎ 212/982–3590). Black, white, and electric colors are the focus here.

TRENDSETTERS

Agnès B. (116 Prince St., ☎ 212/925–4649). This Euro-style boutique has maintained its SoHo popularity for several years.

Charivari (2315 Broadway, between 83rd and 84th Sts., ☎ 212/873–1424). Since Selma Weiser founded this store on the Upper West Side, she has made a name for herself internationally for her eagle eye on the up-and-coming and avant-garde. The branches, too, take a high-style approach: Charivari Sport (201 W. 79th St., ☎ 212/799–8650); Charivari Workshop (441 Columbus Ave., at 81st St., ☎ 212/496–8700); Charivari 72 (257 Columbus Ave., at 72nd St., ☎ 212/787–7272); Charivari 57 (18 W. 57th St., ☎ 212/333–4040); and Charivari on Madison (1001 Madison Ave., at 77th St., ☎ 212/650–0078).

Patricia Field (10 E. 8th St., ☎ 212/254–1699). This store collects the essence of the downtown look.

VINTAGE

Harriet Love (126 Prince St., ☎ 212/966–2280). This is the doyenne of the city's vintage clothing scene.

WOMEN'S SHOES

The shoes at these stores tend toward the classic, in a good range of colors and styles: **Galo** (825 Lexington Ave., at 63rd St., ☎ 212/832–3922; 692 Madison Ave., between 62nd and 63rd Sts., ☎212/688–6276); **Joan & David** (816 Madison Ave., at 68th St., ☎ 212/772–3970; 104 5th Ave., at 16th St., ☎ 212/627–1780); and **Maraolo** (782 Lexington Ave., between 60th and 61st Sts., ☎ 212/832–8182).

Thrift Shops

Everybody's Thrift Shop (261 Park Ave. S, between 20th and 21st Sts., ☎ 212/674–4298).

Housing Works Thrift Shop (141 W. 17th St., ☎ 212/386–0829; and 202 E. 77th St., ☎ 212/772–8461). The newest in New York, these two shops benefit housing services for people with AIDS.

Auctions

New York's lively auction scene means regular sales from internationally known houses. Sales are advertised in the *New York Times,* particularly in Friday's "Weekend" and Sunday's "Arts & Leisure" sections. If you note a sale of interest, attend the exhibition to inspect the wares, peruse the catalogue, discuss possible payment methods, and find out whether you'll need a paddle for bidding.

Christie's (502 Park Ave., at 59th St., ☎ 212/546–1000, 212/371–5438 for recorded schedules). This London firm, more than 200 years old, has had an American presence for more than 15 years. The annex is **Christie's East** (219 E. 67th St., ☎ 212/606–0400).

Sotheby's (1334 York Ave., at 72nd St., ☎ 212/606–7000, 212/606–7245 for recorded schedules). This is Christie's chief rival, also originally from London. Check out the Arcade auctions, where interesting and well-priced also-rans go on the block.

William Doyle Galleries (175 E. 87th St., ☎ 212/427–2730, 212/427–4885 for recorded schedules). The late William Doyle turned his instinct for accumulation into a major force on the New York auction scene.

Flea Markets

The season runs from March or April through November or December at most of these markets in school playgrounds and parking lots.

Annex Antiques Fair and Flea Market (6th Ave., between 24th and 27th Sts., ☎ 212/243–5343), weekends.

The Garage (112 W. 25th St., between 6th and 7th Aves., ☎ 212/647–0707). The newest flea market in town, this one is indoors, in a 23,000-square-foot, two-story former parking garage. Weekends only.

I.S. 44 Market (Columbus Ave., between 76th and 77th Sts., ☎ 212/721–0900 evenings), Sunday.

4 Dining

By J.
Walman

Syndicated
travel,
food, and
wine
journalist
J. Walman
dispenses
culinary
advice to
the 2
million
listeners of
WEVD-
AM.

IN MOST GREAT RESTAURANT TOWNS, there is generally one best restaurant; New York generously offers a variety of candidates. Times being what they are, top restaurants have short lives, chefs play musical kitchens, and today's star is often to-morrow's laggard so temper your visits to famous restaurants with informed selections from among lesser-knowns.

New York gets a bum rap. Of course, you can order caviar and champagne or Bordeaux of great years; you will pay accordingly. But you will also do that in Nashville, Chicago, and Los Angeles. Our point is that each price stratum has its own equilibrium. Translation: $20 is only inexpensive if you get $20 worth of value, and $100 may be a bargain.

If you're watching your budget, always ask the price of the specials, which have become a way for restaurants to charge higher-than-normal prices. Rather than being sensibly at-tached to the menu, European-style, specials are often re-cited by the waiter with no mention of cost. Ask. Finally, always go over your bill. Mistakes do occur (and not al-ways in the restaurant's favor).

Make a reservation. If you change your mind, cancel—it's only courteous. Tables can be hard to come by between 7 and 9; if a restaurant tells you that they can seat you only before 6 or after 10, you may decide that they don't need you. Or you may be persuaded that eating early or late is okay. Eating after a play or concert is quite common in New York, and there's no shortage of options.

CATEGORY	COST*
$$$$	over $60
$$$	$40–$59
$$	$20–$39
$	under $20

*per person, excluding drinks, service, and sales tax (8¼%)

Lower Manhattan

AMERICAN-CONTEMPORARY

$$$ **Hudson River Club.** Spacious and clubby, with river views
★ and soft piano music, it improves with age. Chef Waldy Mal-
ouf celebrates Hudson River Valley produce with his striped
bass with fennel and roasted garlic, rabbit pot pie, and apple-
smoked salmon napoleon with caviar. Desserts like the sig-
nature tower of chocolate—brownie, mousse, and
meringue—are edible sculptures. ✗ 4 *World Financial Cen-
ter,* ☎ *212/786–1500. Reservations required. Jacket and
tie. AE, D, DC, MC, V. No lunch Sat.*

FRENCH

$$$ **Le Pactole.** The Hudson River, which turns gold at night,
makes a breathtaking backdrop to this urbane restaurant,
which boasts spacious seating, burnished cherry wood
chairs, dramatic lighting, and live piano music. Diners can
choose from a short bar menu in the pleasant lounge, traditional French entrées in the stately restaurant, and a
bountiful Sunday brunch buffet, served until 5 PM. ✗ 2 *World
Financial Center,* ☎ *212/945–9444. Reservations required.
AE, DC, MC, V. Closed Sat., Sun. dinner.*

SoHo and TriBeCa

AMERICAN-CONTEMPORARY

$$$$ **American Renaissance.** A dramatic staircase leads from
★ the casual café on the first level (where you can sample the
flavored vodkas) to the stunning main dining room with
its cascading waterfall, Beaux-Arts ornamentation, and
23-foot ceiling supported by Ionic columns. Roasted Atlantic salmon, glazed in vintage port with shaved aspara-
gus and tahini-lime dressing might serve as the prelude to
New York state organic fallow venison served with roasted
wild chestnuts, celery leaves, gooseberry juice, and apple
oil. ✗ 260 *West Broadway (at Erickson Pl.),* ☎ *212/343–
0049. Reservations suggested. AE, DC, MC, V. Lunch:
weekdays. Closed Sat. lunch, Sun.*

$$$$ **Bouley.** In this striking TriBeCa room with vaulted ceilings,
wildflower bouquets, and impressionistic paintings, your
tab is one of the city's most elevated. A special lunch *de-
gustation* (tasting) menu offers astonishing value. Alaskan

spot prawn ravioli with fresh New Orleans shrimp, Maine baby pink shrimp, sea scallops, Cape Cod mussels, and herbal broth demonstrate not only Chef David Bouley's penchant for fresh regional products, but also an underlying complexity of style. ✕ *165 Duane St., between Greenwich and Hudson Sts.,* ☏ *212/608–3852. Jacket and tie. AE, DC, MC, V. Closed Sat. lunch, Sun.*

$$ **Match.** This bilevel restaurant-lounge is hot enough to scorch the heels of a seasoned fire-walker. Check out the raw bar, which teems with fabulous presentations of fresh shellfish, sushi, and caviar, or go for the dim sum platter. Entrées range from burgers (ham, turkey, or tuna) to more innovative options like duck pizza and steak frites with a caramelized shallot sauce. And if you're in the mood for entertainment after all this feasting, head for the music in the downstairs club. ✕ *160 Mercer St., between Houston and Prince Sts.,* ☏ *212/343–0020. Reservations suggested. AE, MC, V.*

$$ **Nosmo King.** The name of this TriBeCan, a play on the phrase "no smoking," is not its only quirk. It's all deliciously eccentric. There are crystal chandeliers and watermelon margaritas, fresh-squeezed juices, and organic wines. Nothing on the fascinating menu is run-of-the-mill—sweet potato and black bean quesadillas; beet, goat cheese, and potato tart; and spicy duck ragout with hominy corn bread and collard greens. ✕ *54 Varick St., south of Canal St.,* ☏ *212/ 966–1239. Reservations advised. AE, DC, MC, V. No lunch weekends.*

FRENCH

$$$ **Montrachet.** This TriBeCa trendsetter is unpretentious in its decor: pastel walls, plush mauve banquettes, and engaging works of art. A satisfying dinner might begin with Taylor bay scallops in the shell with tomatoes and fresh herbs, followed by roasted veal kidney in sherry vinegar sauce, and one (or more) of the noteworthy desserts: banana and chocolate gratin over linzer crust or pumpkin mascarpone cream with a sauce made of dried cranberries. ✕ *239 W. Broadway, between Walker and White Sts.,* ☏ *212/219–2777. Reservations a must. AE. Closed Sun.; no lunch Mon.–Thurs. or Sat.*

FRENCH BISTRO

$–$$ Felix. No, you haven't traveled 3,000 miles to Paris's Left Bank; this charming bistro is in SoHo, a taxi ride from midtown. Try the chicken or rabbit fricassee; the brioche with raspberry coulis and frozen apple pudding make satisfying exits. There's brunch on Sunday. ✕ *340 W. Broadway, at Grand St.,* ☎ *212/431–0021. AE. Closed Mon. lunch.*

MEXICAN

$$ El Teddy's. The margaritas need only a bit more lime to be perfect, and the food is mostly wonderful, revealing both authentic Mexican subtleties and contemporary creativity, from the fabulous salsa and roasted corn soup to the smoked chicken and goat-cheese quesadilla and the pork, chicken, and fruit stew. The roster of inventive desserts includes summer bread pudding and chocolate tamales— odd-sounding but yummy. ✕ *219 W. Broadway, between Franklin and White Sts.,* ☎ *212/941–7070. Reservations advised. AE, MC, V. No lunch weekends.*

THAI

$ Kin Khao. Hip downtowners have already discovered this inventive Thai restaurant in SoHo. It's jam-packed—and worth the wait. The masterful *gai tom kha,* a traditional soup with chicken, coconut milk, mushrooms, and ginger, says it all; the kitchen here understands balance. Try the superb red snapper with sweet-and-sour chili sauce or the complex green curry with chicken. Sticky rice is heaven; for dessert, it comes with sesame seeds and fresh mango. ✕ *171 Spring St., between W. Broadway and Thompson St.,* ☎ *212/966–3939. Reservations only for 6 or more. AE, MC, V. No lunch.*

Chinatown, Little Italy, East Village, and Lower East Side

AMERICAN

$ First. Inner-city flavor, late-night dining, and fabulous food! The prices are rock-bottom considering the quality. Gazpacho with jumbo shrimp, presented in a salted-rim martini-glass, is spectacular, as is the grilled steak with blue cheese and a side dish with every vegetable on the list. Try the remarkable warm chocolate pudding cake with coffee ice cream. ✕ *87 1st Ave., between 5th and 6th Sts.,* ☏ *212/674–3823. Reservations advised. AE, DC, MC, V. Dinner only.*

CANTONESE

\$–\$\$ **Triple Eight Palace.** This quintessential Hong Kong–style em-
★ porium is wild and wonderful—loud and jam-packed with
Chinese families (and lots of babies). It's also one of the
pleasantest spots for dim sum. Try shrimp in phyllo, turnip
cake, spicy squid, steamed pork buns, crab claws, and
steamed and fried dumplings. In the evening, you can order
excellent seafood, Cantonese specialties, and noodle dishes.
✕ *78 E. Broadway, between Division and Market Sts.,* ☏
*212/941–8886. Reservations only for 6 or more. AE, DC,
MC, V.*

DELI

\$ **Second Avenue Deli.** Here it is, the last of a dying breed.
Brusque service, leviathan sandwiches, matzo-ball soup,
chopped liver—they're alive and well at the Second Avenue
Deli. Try it, you'll like it. ✕ *156 2nd Ave., at 10th St.,* ☏
212/677–0606. No reservations. AE.

ITALIAN

\$\$ **S.P.Q.R.** This inviting spot with spacious tables and lots of
fresh flowers is one of the few earnest restaurants in Little
Italy, an area more noted for fun than food. In addition to
the good pasta, there's a terrific veal chop and the signa-
ture homemade cheesecake. ✕ *133 Mulberry St., between
Hester and Grand Sts.,* ☏ *212/925–3120. Reservations ad-
vised. AE, DC, MC, V.*

JAPANESE

\$ **Takahachi.** One of the best small Japanese restaurants in
★ Manhattan, it's neat and amazingly inexpensive, offering
such unusual dishes as fried shiitake mushrooms filled with
ground salmon, chopped tuna sashimi with scallions, seared
tuna with black pepper and mustard sauce, and grilled
chicken stuffed with plum paste and siso leaf. There's also
a good early-bird special, served until 7 PM. Wine and beer
only. ✕ *85 Ave. A, between 5th and 6th Sts.,* ☏ *212/505–
6524. No reservations. AE, MC, V. No lunch.*

LATIN AMERICAN

$ **Boca Chica.** This raffish East Villager, hot as a firecracker,
★   has live music, dancing, and assertively seasoned food from
several Latin American nations at giveaway prices. Check
out the soupy Puerto Rican chicken-rice stew known as
asopao, Cuban sandwiches, Bolivian sweet corn topped with
chicken, and the nurturing rice pudding. Try a potent
caipirinha (lime juice and Brazilian rum). Don't trip over
the boa constrictor by the bar. ✗ *13 1st Ave. near 1st St.,*
☎ *212/473–0108. No reservations. AE, DC, MC, V. No
lunch Mon.–Sat.*

SEAFOOD

$ **Pisces.** At this striking restaurant, where tables near the
★   open windows seem to spill out into Alphabet City, as this
neighborhood of lettered avenues is called, $15 buys an
outstanding three-course dinner. Such sophisticated dishes
as smoked salmon terrine with adobo sauce, and grilled
tuna hidden under a tower of fried onions, are incongru-
ous to the East Village scene, but after a delicious dessert
it doesn't seem to matter. ✗ *95 Ave. A, at 6th St.,* ☎ *212/
260–6660. Reservations advised. AE, MC, V. No lunch
weekdays.*

Greenwich Village

AMERICAN-CONTEMPORARY

$$$ **Gotham Bar & Grill.** Will success spoil this innovator? Ap-
★   parently not, since management keeps careful watch over
the service (generally excellent) and the kitchen (always in-
ventive; it was chef Alfred Portale who originated the ver-
tical style of food presentation, which turns each plate into
an artful edible tower). Try the sublime Gotham pasta,
which is composed and priced daily, or the monkfish tail,
accompanied by savoy cabbage, smoked bacon, creamed
potatoes, flageolets, and foie-gras ravioli. The wine list is
intelligent, and the lofty, multilevel space was the proto-
type of the new-style New York restaurant. ✗ *12 E. 12th
St.,* ☎ *212/620–4020. Reservations advised. AE, DC, MC,
V. No lunch weekends.*

FRENCH BISTRO

$–$$ **L'Auberge Du Midi.** If you want the "perfect Greenwich Village restaurant," look no further than this seductive bistro. The welcome couldn't be more ingratiating, and the food is relatively inexpensive and honest, including sea scallops with leeks in champagne sauce (among several carefully prepared seafood dishes), roast rack of lamb with fresh thyme, bouillabaisse on Friday (chef Jean Roger is from Marseilles), or the couscous of Madame's native Fez, delicious under its typical garnish of caramelized onions. ✕ *310 W. 4th St., between W. 12th and Bank Sts.,* ☎ *212/242–4705. Reservations advised. AE, MC, V. Closed Mon. Nov.–Mar.; no lunch.*

PIZZA

$ **Arturo's.** Few guidebooks list this brick-walled Village landmark, but the body-to-body crowds teetering on the wobbly wooden chairs suggest good things. The pizza is terrific, cooked in a coal-fired oven; if you want the works, order the Fiesta combo. Basic pastas as well as seafood, veal, and chicken concoctions with mozzarella and lots of tomato sauce come at giveaway prices. ✕ *106 W. Houston St., off Thompson St.,* ☎ *212/677–3820. No reservations. AE, MC, V.*

Gramercy Park, Murray Hill, Chelsea, and the Flatiron District

AMERICAN-CONTEMPORARY

$$$ **Gramercy Tavern.** A 91-foot Robert Kushner mural of fruit and vegetables wraps around the bar. The dining areas are reminiscent of an English tavern, with white-washed walls, arched doorways, wrought-iron grillwork, and vaulted ceilings. The menu has an eclectic, Mediterranean feel that's best represented by the fresh seafood and game dishes, many of which sparkle with such unusual vegetable accompaniments as pickled ramps or roasted fennel. ✕ *42 E. 20th St., between Broadway and Park Ave. S,* ☎ *212/ 477–0777. Reservations advised. AE, DC, MC, V. No lunch weekends.*

$$$ **Union Square Café.** Breads are delicious, and appetizers sparkle—we heartily endorse iced oysters on the half shell, shucked to order, with shallot vinaigrette. While dinner entrées are good, the sandwiches served at lunch—for example, fresh-tuna salad on Tom Cat white bread with slab bacon, arugula, and garlic potato chips—are heavenly. Desserts are winners and include caramel, pecan, and chocolate ice cream tartufo and an old-fashioned apple cobbler à la mode with orange walnut raisin sauce. ✘ *21 E. 16th St.,* ☎ *212/243–4020. Reservations required. AE, DC, MC, V. No lunch Sun.*

AUSTRIAN

$ **Kaffeehaus.** This café-cum-restaurant with its upholstered banquettes, marble-top tables, pastry display, and racks of newspapers and magazines, recreates old Vienna. There's also an inviting neighborhood feeling—not to mention terrific Viennese coffee *mit schlag* (with cream), *caffè latte* (espresso with steamed milk), unusual organic and unfiltered wheat beers, interesting Austrian wines, and food that will surprise you with its finesse. Start with dilled smoked salmon tartare on *rösti* (roast potatoes) or smoked trout with beets and horseradish cream. Then go for a classic pork Wienerschnitzel, eastern Austrian fish stew, or pan-roasted lake trout in cucumber dill sauce. ✘ *131 8th Ave., between 16th and 17th Sts.,* ☎ *212/229–9702. Reservations advised. DC, MC, V.*

ITALIAN

$$$ **Le Madri.** The Tuscan-style space with vaulted ceiling and
★ wood-burning pizza oven is the creation of Pino Luango (of Coco Pazzo). Depending on how you choose, your meal could be either robust (fried calamari with spicy roast pepper-tomato sauce), homey (braised veal shank with portobello mushrooms and saffron risotto), or elegant (fettuccine with lobster, shrimp, and butternut squash). Desserts include walnut and fig ricotta cake with chocolate sauce, and vanilla gelato. ✘ *168 W. 18th St.,* ☎ *212/727–8022. Reservations advised. AE, DC, MC, V.*

LATIN-CONTEMPORARY

$$$ **Patria.** This trendy trilevel Caribbean café is owned by
★ Phillip Suarez (of Vong and Jo Jo). Apparently Mr. Suarez can do no wrong: Note the Honduran conch chowder; shrimp in Ecuadorian peanut stew with green tomato salsa; braised oxtail in Rioja sauce with green rice; and the sig-

nature dessert, a chocolate-filled cigar with spice-bread ice cream. The service is as excellent as the food; the wine list focuses on Spain, Argentina, and California. ✗ *250 Park Ave. S, at 20th St.,* ☎ *212/777-6211. Reservations required. AE, MC, V.*

SPANISH-CONTEMPORARY

$$ **Bolo.** The food aims at New York palates: A typically Spanish roasted marinated shrimp with toasted garlic comes with a contemporary flatbread garnish, and curried-shellfish paella unites bivalves with sausage, chicken, and rice. Other treats: grilled octopus and white bean salad stuffed in a caramelized onion, salt-cod-and-potato fritters, and trendy burnt orange-chocolate flan with cinnamon syrup. The house sangria is perfect. ✗ *23 E. 22nd St.,* ☎ *212/228–2200. Reservations advised. AE, MC, V. Closed Sat. lunch, Sun.*

Midtown

AMERICAN-CONTEMPORARY

$$$$ **The "21" Club.** Service here is seamless and pampering, and
★ it's exhilarating to hobnob with celebrities and tycoons and sip a well-made cocktail served by what feels like your own butler. Executive chef Michael Lomonaco can knock out creditable renditions of the signature "21" burger and chicken hash, but also finesses the more complex culinary challenges of such dishes as his barely cooked scallops, encased in a crackling sesame-seed crust, garnished with a single potato chip bearing fresh Sevruga caviar. Desserts are not strong. ✗ *21 W. 52nd St.,* ☎ *212/582–7200. Reservations required. Jacket and tie. AE, DC, MC, V. Closed Sat. lunch, Sun.*

FRENCH-THAI

$$ **Vong.** Most of the food is very good—don't miss the lobster and daikon roll with rosemary-ginger dip, the rabbit curry braised with carrots and cumin seed, or the coconut soup with chicken and *galanga,* an herb that gives special character to Thai cuisine. Lychee and papaya soup and banana, kiwi, and passion fruit salad with white pepper ice cream stand out. ✗ *200 E. 54th St.,* ☎ *212/486–9592. Reservations required. AE, DC, MC, V. No lunch weekends.*

INDIAN

$$
★ **Dāwat.** One of the city's finest Indians, this classy, understated spot has flattering lighting, smooth service, and a menu full of consultant Madhur Jaffrey's subtle cuisine: shrimp in mustard seeds with curry leaves, lamb with white turnips, black-eyed peas and corn, and onion *kulcha*—an onion-stuffed bread flavored with fresh coriander. Dāwat demonstrates the charms of Indian sweets; try the pudding-like carrot halva. ✗ *210 E. 58th St.,* ☎ *212/355–7555. Reservations advised. AE, DC, MC, V. No lunch Sun.*

JAPANESE

$$$$ **Seryna.** This lovely restaurant vividly evokes Tokyo with its dignified air, comfortable seating, and understated colors. Although the sushi is superbly fresh, the specialty is steak Ishiyaki, cooked tableside on a smoldering rock. Cocktails are served in small carafes that come buried in crushed ice. Service is superb. ✗ *11 E. 53rd St.,* ☎ *212/980–9393. Reservations advised. AE, DC, MC, V. Closed Sat. lunch, Sun.*

KOREAN

$
★ **New York Kom Tang Soot Bul House.** This is the best Korean restaurant on a street jammed with them, and dinner is a show. So come ready for charades (little English is spoken); wear clothes you don't mind getting smoky (from the hibachis in the center of the communal tables); and insist on the attractive second floor. Dinner starts with ten delicious sides, including kim chee, the fiery Korean pickle. ✗ *32 W. 32nd St.,* ☎ *212/947–8482. Reservations: difficult if you don't speak Korean. AE, MC, V.*

STEAK

$$$–$$$$ **Smith & Wollensky.** This archetypal New York–style member of the club, with its bold setting, gargantuan portions, and lofty list of wines is one of the best. Meat is dry-aged in-house, and sirloin, porterhouse, and double sirloin (our test of a fine steak house) arrive cooked to a turn. The bustling, less-pricey Wollensky's Grill next door shares the main restaurant's carnivorous bias, but has pleasant sidewalk seating in summer. ✗ *201 E. 49th St.,* ☎ *212/753–1530 (Grill* ☎ *212/753–0444). Reservations advised. AE, DC, MC, V. No lunch weekends in restaurant.*

VIETNAMESE

$$–$$$ **Le Colonial.** The dining room here is straight out of Somerset Maugham with its rattan chairs, potted palms, ceiling fans, shutters, and black-and-white period photographs. Start with the superb *bahn cuon*, steamed Vietnamese ravioli with chicken, shrimp, and mushrooms, and move on to crisp-fried whole snapper. Sorbets, ice creams, and fruit-based puddings are right on. Don't miss the Vietnamese coffee—strong black brew over a layer of condensed milk. ✕ *149 E. 57th St.,* ☎ *212/752–0808. Reservations advised. AE, DC, MC, V.*

Theater District and Carnegie Hall

DELI

$ **Carnegie Deli.** Although not what it was, this no-nonsense spot is still one of midtown's two best delis, a species distinguished by crowds, noise, impatient service, and jumbo sandwiches. Try to get the counterman to hand-slice your corned beef or pastrami; the extra juiciness and superior texture warrant the extra charge. ✕ *854 7th Ave., between 54th and 55th Sts.,* ☎ *212/757–2245. No reservations. No credit cards.*

FRENCH

$$$–$$$$ **Petrossian.** With its abundance of marble, this art deco caviar
★ bar and restaurant is like no other New York dining spot. A tasting dinner starts with gobs of fresh beluga on buttered toast (with no competing garnishes); then comes a huge, perfectly roasted scallop, lovely braised salmon, or tender sautéed veal; and you end with a seductive chocolate soufflé or homemade ice cream. Have vodka with the caviar or champagne throughout. ✕ *182 W. 58th St.,* ☎ *212/245–2214. Reservations advised. AE, DC, MC, V.*

GREEK

$ **Uncle Nick's.** This unpretentious taverna is best at simple grills: baby octopus or whole red snapper, porgy, or sea bass on the bone. The Greek country salad will delight you. The *saganakityri*, a sharp cheese baked in lemon butter and flamed, is delicious, as is yogurt drizzled with honey. Skip the spongy baklava. ✕ *747 9th Ave., between 50th and 51st Sts.,* ☎ *212/315–1726. MC, V.*

Dining Uptown

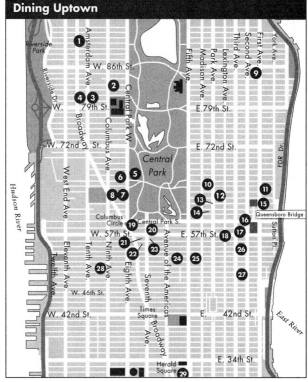

Amsterdam's, **4**

Arizona, **16**

Aureole, **14**

Café des Artistes, **6**

Carmine's, **1**

Carnegie Deli, **22**

Dāwat, **17**

Fujiyama Mama, **2**

Jo Jo, **12**

L'Auberge, **11**

Le Cirque, **10**

Le Colonial, **18**

New York Kom
Tang Soot Bul
House, **29**

Park Avenue
Café, **13**

Petrossian, **20**

Picholine, **7**

The Pie, **9**

Russian Tea
Room, **23**

San Domenico, **19**

Sarabeth's
Kitchen, **3**

Seryna, **25**

Shun Lee West, **8**

Smith &
Wollensky, **27**

Sushi Hatsu, **15**

Tavern on the
Green, **5**

Trattoria
dell'Arte, **21**

The "21" Club, **24**

Uncle Nick's, **28**

Vong, **26**

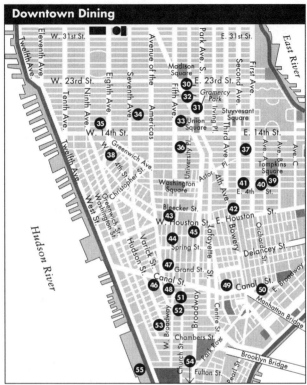

Downtown Dining

ITALIAN

$$$–$$$$ **San Domenico.** Executive chef Theo Schoenegger executes
★ with authority such dishes as Mediterranean baby cuttle-
fish with vegetables, soft egg-yolk ravioli with truffle but-
ter, and roast baby goat; for dessert, try the custard with
balsamic vinegar and caramel sauce or cornmeal-chocolate
soufflé. The setting is like a private villa, with terra-cotta
floors, sumptuous leather chairs, and lots of warm, earthy
hues. ✗ *240 Central Park S,* ☎ *212/265–5959. Reserva-
tions required. Jacket and tie except on Sun. AE, MC, DC,
V. No lunch weekends.*

$$ **Trattoria dell'Arte.** This top trattoria still displays the con-
★ troversial oversize renderings of body parts. But the real
draw nowadays is the delicious cuisine, as in the marvelous
penne with grilled vegetables and calamari, the linguini with
red bean sauce and shiitake mushrooms, and the incredi-
ble whole fish with green olives and white wine. Double
veal chops are mammoth, desserts fabulous. Weekends,
there's brunch. ✗ *900 7th Ave., between 56th and 57th Sts.,*
☎ *212/245–9800. Reservations advised. AE, DC, MC, V.*

RUSSIAN

$$$ **Russian Tea Room.** Everybody's favorite tea room is mak-
ing a stellar attempt to get into the serious-kitchen busi-
ness. Predictably, blini and caviar with a selection from one
of the most extensive vodka lists in town is perfect. Less
predictably, traditional Russian borscht and beef Stroganoff
are less successful than such nouvelle creations as grilled
sea scallops and rock shrimp surrounding a gâteau made
of blini, with Ossetra caviar and lemon-vodka sauce. ✗ *150
W. 57th St.,* ☎ *212/265–0947. Reservations advised. Jacket
required at dinner. AE, DC, MC, V.*

Upper East Side

AMERICAN-CONTEMPORARY

$$$$ **Aureole.** Along with Bouley, Charles Palmer's fashionable,
beautiful restaurant is one of the town's toughest reserva-
tions. Appetizers are generally reliable; desserts are visual
masterpieces. Wine prices are high, and the ventilation and
ambience upstairs are sub-par. ✗ *34 E. 61st St.,* ☎ *212/319–*

1660. Reservations required. AE, DC, MC, V. Closed Sat. lunch, Sun.

$$$ Park Avenue Café. American folk art, antique toys, and sheafs of dried wheat decorate this unpretentious pacesetter. A delicate flan of celeriac and foie gras comes in an eggshell held by a porcelain bunny; salmon is cured like pastrami and arrives on a marble cylinder, and the signature swordfish "chop" is dressed with a numbered tag (save the tag, sign the book and you may win a first-class trip to Paris). A desert selection of petit fours and handmade chocolates is presented on an antique toy stove. ✕ *100 E. 63rd St.,* ☎ *212/644–1900. Reservations advised. AE, DC, MC, V. Closed Sat., lunch.*

$$ **Jo Jo.** At this chic spot, Chef Jean-Georges Vongerichten
★ concentrates on carefully executing traditional bistro classics with contemporary touches. Most of his creations are impressive, including such dishes as sweetbreads with chestnut-truffle vinaigrette, scallops with chopped raw beets and parsley juice, and pork cheeks and black-bean salad. ✕ *160 E. 64th St.,* ☎ *212/223–5656. Reservations required. AE, MC, V. Closed Sat. lunch, Sun.*

FRENCH

$$$$ Le Cirque. The rich, the famous, and dentists from Des Moines all want to dine at this palace of international luxury; one comes here not to eat but for the experience. Savor the signature crème brûlée (Le Cirque put this king of custards on the international culinary map). The wine list is encyclopedic and tolerably priced. ✕ *58 E. 65th St.,* ☎ *212/794–9292. Reservations required. Jacket and tie. AE, DC, MC, V. Closed Sun.*

JAPANESE

$$$$ Sushi Hatsu. For sushi, sashimi, and meticulously prepared fresh fish—here's the city's best. Insist on sitting at the sushi bar (to the right, as you enter; ignore the "reserved" sign). Try a thin egg crepe filled with sushi, tied like a beggar's purse, and topped with fish roe (one of the few affordable items). And beyond that, just point to what appeals to you in the glass case. Drink steaming cups of green tea, or icy Japanese draft beer. ✕ *1143 1st Ave., between 62nd and 63rd Sts.,* ☎ *212/371–0238. No reservations. AE, MC, V.*

MIDDLE EASTERN

$ L'Auberge. With its flattering lighting and elegant decor, L'Auberge recalls Paris more than Beirut. You'll know it's Lebanese when you dig into the delicious hummus and *kibbee* (ground lamb). Go with a group and sample the assorted *mezze* (appetizers). The $6.95 all-you-can-eat weekday lunch buffet is a steal. ✕ *1191 1st Ave., between 64th and 65th Sts.,* ☎ *212/288–8791. Reservations accepted. AE, DC, MC, V.*

RUSSIAN

$ The Pie. This pint-size slice of Russia, transplanted to a
★ Yorkville storefront, specializes in Russian pies, made from crepes arranged in a casserole and bursting with your choice of filling. Blini with herring, salmon caviar, and smoked salmon are divine appetizers. Soups are honest and satisfying. Entrées include filet mignon pie, and chicken Rasputin in a spicy tomato sauce on noodles. ✕ *340 E. 86th St.,* ☎ *212/517–8717. Reservations advised. AE.*

SOUTHWESTERN

$$–$$$ Arizona 206. Stucco walls and blanched wood create a desert look here and at the less expensive adjacent Arizona Café. But no Mojave truck stop serves dishes like green chili corncakes with tequila-cured salmon, salmon roe, and iced El Tesoro Plata. And the spicy grilled rabbit in cilantro oil, with the braised leg served in a crisp tortilla, is obligatory. If you dare, try the pumpkin custard, which is layered with pumpkin-seed crisps and caramelized dates. ✕ *206 E. 60th St.,* ☎ *212/838–0440. AE, DC, MC, V. No Sun. lunch.*

Lincoln Center

AMERICAN-CONTEMPORARY

$$$ Tavern on the Green. The reception is perfunctory, the service inept (if usually polite), and the food still hit or miss. Nevertheless, Warner LeRoy's lavish restaurant is a visual fantasy, and careful selection can yield a satisfying meal. There's also jazz, dancing, and cabaret. Request the brilliant Crystal Room for its view of the twinkle-lighted trees. ✕ *In Central Park, at 67th St.,* ☎ *212/873–3200. Reservations advised. AE, DC, MC, V.*

CHINESE

$$ **Shun Lee West.** It's a dramatically lighted study in black, accented by white dragons and monkeys. Try Peking duck, sweetbreads with hot peppers and scallions, or rack of lamb Szechuan style. Fresh fruit makes an ideal dessert. ✕ *43 W. 65th St.,* ☎ *212/595–8895. Reservations advised. AE, DC, MC, V.*

FRENCH

$$$ **Café des Artistes.** Writer–restaurant consultant George
★ Lang's masterpiece, this most European of cafés is snug and beautiful with its polished oak woodwork and rosy Howard Chandler Christy murals of nymphs at play. The cuisine is as refined as the setting—it would be hard to find a better *pot au feu,* a French variation on pot roast. The Sunday brunch is especially festive. ✕ *1 W. 67th St.,* ☎ *212/877– 3500. Reservations required. Jacket and tie required at dinner. AE, DC, MC, V.*

MEDITERRANEAN

$$ **Picholine.** Dried flowers, plaid fabrics, and rough stucco cre-
★ ate a rustic look here. The whole roasted fish for two, filleted table-side, is not to be slighted, nor is the toothsome duck risotto with wild mushrooms, pumpkin, and white truffle oil. Assorted housemade cookies add an upright finishing touch. ✕ *35 W. 64th St., between Broadway and Central Park W,* ☎ *212/724–8585. Reservations advised. AE, DC, MC, V. Closed Mon. lunch, Sun.*

Upper West Side

AMERICAN-CASUAL

$ **Amsterdam's.** Tables under the checkered cloths in this unpretentious bistro often need a matchbook, chairs are none too comfortable, and the noise challenges conversation. But the food is reliable and tasty. The house antipasto for two includes a delicious Italian *crostini,* firm toast spread with chicken-liver pâté. ✕ *428 Amsterdam Ave., between 80th and 81st Sts.,* ☎ *212/874–1377. AE, MC, V. Closed Mon. lunch.*

AMERICAN-CONTEMPORARY

$$ **Sarabeth's Kitchen.** Despite the bric-a-brac and homespun charm, this is no mere tea room. An innovative tomato soup with bits of fresh tomato, cream, and fresh dill, and quality sirloin steak, sweet-potato hash, and greens attest to that. ✗ *423 Amsterdam Ave., between 80th and 81st Sts., ☎ 212/ 496–6280; 1295 Madison Ave., between 92nd and 93rd Sts., ☎ 212/410–7335. Reservations advised. AE, MC, V.*

ITALIAN

$–$$ **Carmine's.** Dark woodwork and old-fashioned black-and-
★ white tiles make this hot spot look like an old-timer. Kick off a meal with homemade mozzarella-tomato salad and move on to the pastas, perhaps rigatoni in a rollicking broccoli, sausage, and white bean sauce. Wines are inexpensive. ✗ *2450 Broadway, between 90th and 91st Sts., ☎ 212/362–2200. Reservations only for 6 or more. AE. Dinner only.*

JAPANESE

$$ **Fujiyama Mama.** White-slipcover side chairs line up like statues in the vitrine of this creative restaurant with a high-tech design. Dishes have names like Poseidon Adventure and Bermuda Triangle. But the food is serious, inventive, and invariably first-rate, including marinated chicken in a blue curaçao sauce and sparkling tuna, fluke, yellow tail, sea trout, and salmon sushi, sashimi, and hand rolls. ✗ *467 Columbus Ave., between 82nd and 83rd Sts., ☎ 212/769–1144. Reservations advised. AE. No lunch.*

Worth A Special Trip

AMERICAN-CONTEMPORARY

$$$$ **River Café.** Sipping a cocktail or a glass of wine from the
★ extensive list and watching the sun set over Lower Manhattan, just across the East River, is one of the city's most romantic restaurants. Favorite dishes include fruitwood-smoked salmon on johnnycake; a remarkable poached salmon in a ginger, green onion, and lime-leaf broth; and halibut fillet in rice paper with braised mushrooms and Thompson grapes. ✗ *1 Water St., at the East River, Brooklyn, ☎ 718/522– 5200. Reservations advised. AE, DC, MC, V.*

Coffee Bars and Cafés

Book Friends Cafe (16 W. 18th St., ☎ 212/255–7407); **Caffè Reggio** (119 MacDougal St., ☎ 212/475–9557); **Caffè Vivaldi** (32 Jones St., near Bleecker St., ☎ 212/929–9384); **Cafe Word of Mouth** (1012 Lexington Ave., between 72nd and 73rd Sts., ☎ 212/249–5351); **Edgar's** (255 W. 84th St., ☎ 212/496–6126).

5 Lodging

By Jane
Hershey

Updated
by Kate
Sekules

IF ANY SINGLE ELEMENT of your trip to New York City is going to cost you a lot of money, it'll be your hotel bill. European cities may offer plenty of low-priced lodgings, but New York tends not to. Real estate is at a premium here, and labor costs are high, so hoteliers start out with a lot of expenses to cover. And there are enough well-heeled visitors to support competition at the premium end of the spectrum, which is where the profits are. Fleabags and flophouses aside, there's precious little here for under $100 a night. The city no longer has the highest hotel tax in the country (that distinction belongs to Columbus, Ohio), but you should not fail to figure in the 15¼% combined taxes when calculating what your temporary bed will cost. We have scoured the city for good-value hotels and budget properties, but even our "Inexpensive" category includes hotels that run as high as $135 for one night's stay in a double.

It's important to realize, however, that our price categories are based on the "rack rate," or the standard room cost that hotels print in their brochures and quote over the phone. You almost never need pay this much. If you book directly with the hotel, try asking for the corporate rate, any seasonal special offers, or weekend deals. The latter typically include extras, like complimentary meals, drinks, or tickets to events. Of course, booking any all-inclusive package, weekend or longer, will reduce the hotel rate.

Cost is not the sole consideration when it comes to finding lodgings in New York, though. How you feel relaxing in your hotel room makes a vast difference to how much energy you have for your mission in the Big Apple. We have checked out the hotels in these pages for security and cleanliness, but location is up to you. If you intend to walk Museum Mile, pick the Upper East side; if you like to see trees and opera, stay close to Lincoln Center; if razzmatazz turns you on, go for theaterland; or for peaceful nights, try Murray Hill. Within each price category, our listings are organized by neighborhood. In general, Manhattan hotels don't measure up to those in other U.S. cities in terms of room size, parking, or outside landscaping. But, this being a sophisticated city,

Manhattan Lodging

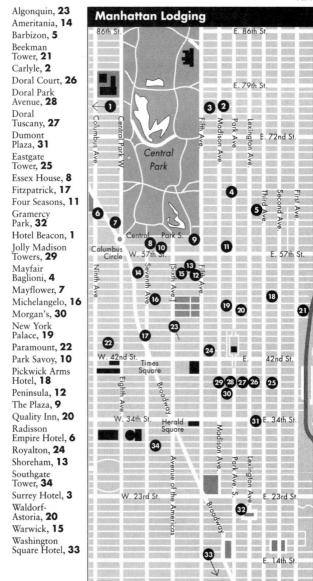

New York hotels usually compensate with fastidious service, sprucely maintained properties, and restaurants that hold their own in a city of knowledgeable diners.

Note: Even the most exclusive hotels have security gaps. Be discreet with valuables everywhere, and stay alert in public areas.

New York is constantly full of vacationers, conventioneers, and business travelers, all requiring hotel space. Try to book your room as far in advance as possible, using a major credit card to guarantee the reservation; you might even want to work through a travel agent.

CATEGORY	COST*
$$$$	over $260
$$$	$190–$260
$$	$135–$190
$	under $135

All prices are for a standard double room, excluding 15¼% city and state taxes.

Unless otherwise noted in the individual descriptions, all the hotels listed have the following features and services: private baths, central heating, air-conditioning, private telephones, on-premises dining, valet and room service (though not necessarily 24-hour or short-notice), TV (including cable and pay-per-view films), and a routine concierge staff. Larger hotels will generally have video or high-speed checkout capability. Pools are a rarity, but most properties have fitness centers; we note only those that are on the premises, but other hotels usually have arrangements for guests at nearby facilities, for which a fee is sometimes charged.

$$$$

★ **The Carlyle.** Museum Mile and the tony boutiques of Madison Avenue are on the doorstep of New York's least hysterical grand hotel, where European tradition and Manhattan swank shake hands. The mood is English manor house; larger rooms and suites, many of them decorated by the famous interior designer Mark Hampton, have terraces, pantries, and antique furnishings. Baths, though more subdued than others in town, are marble and chock-full of de rigueur amenities such as hair dryers, fine toiletries, and makeup mirrors. Most visitors have heard about the famous Café Carlyle, where performers such as Bobby Short entertain. But the hotel also contains the charming Bemelman's Bar, named after Ludwig Bemelman, illustrator of the beloved children's book character Madeline and the "twelve little girls in two straight lines"; he created the murals here as well as in the formal Carlyle Restaurant, known for French cuisine and old-fashioned courtly service. There's a jewel of a fitness center that is ultraprivate and luxurious. This is one of the few grand hotels where friendliness and old-school elegance really mix; you don't have to be a famous face to get a smile or good treatment. The concierge and housekeeping service is especially excellent. ☎ *35 E. 76th St., 10021, ☎ 212/744–1600, ℻ 212/717–4682. 190 rooms. Restaurant, bar, café, lobby lounge, kitchenettes and pantries in larger units, exercise room, meeting rooms. AE, DC, MC, V.*

★ **Essex House.** The owners, Japan's Nikko Hotels, have done wonders for this stately Central Park South property. The public interiors are an Art Deco masterpiece fit for Fred and Ginger. Journey's, the hotel's wood-paneled bar, has a working fireplace. The delights continue upstairs, where guest rooms and baths resemble those in a splendid English country home. The staff is discreet, efficient, and friendly. This is the place to take advantage of weekend rates and book that dreamed-about suite on the park. ☎ *160 Central Park S (near 7th Ave.), 10019, ☎ 212/247–0300, ℻ 212/315–1839. 593 rooms. 3 restaurants, bar, health club, meeting rooms, business center. AE, DC, MC, V.*

The Four Seasons. If you shop at Barneys and prefer Woody Allen's Ingmar Bergman imitations to his comedies, you'll love New York's tallest, newest, most expensive hotel. I. M. Pei—he of the Louvre Pyramid, among other modernist icons—designed this limestone-clad, stepped spire amid the prime shops of 57th Street, and he made it big. The guest rooms are big (600 square feet on average) and the lobby is bigger than big. Leading into the aptly named Grand Foyer, it is dauntingly sky high, and its French limestone pillars, marble, onyx, and acre upon acre of blonde wood are a study in earth-toned elegance.

What could possibly justify the astronomical rates? Gleaming English sycamore dressing areas with a giant mirror perhaps, and enough closets to hold a year's worth of clothing. Well-stocked fridges, security entry locks, beige blackout drapes you operate by bedside button, and high-quality modern art on the flesh-colored walls are further classy touches. The boring house toiletries don't measure up. Wear Armani, Gucci, or Lauren, or you'll feel out of place. And bring your own color. ☎ *57 E. 57th St.,* ☎ *212/758–5700,* FAX *212/758–5711. 367 rooms. Restaurant, bar, lounge café, sauna, spa, health club, business services, meeting rooms. AE, DC, MC, V.*

The Mayfair Baglioni. General manager Dario Mariotti adds a cheery Italian influence to this low-key, gracious hotel. Locals know it for its traditional tea lounge and its first-rate restaurant, Le Cirque (*see* Chapter 4). Even the smallest of the guest rooms has marble baths and traditional-style, peach-tone decor with up-to-date extras such as dual-line telephones and outlets to accommodate portable computers and fax machines. Service is superefficient; guests are offered umbrellas, room humidifiers, customized pillow selection, and the ingenuity of longtime concierge Bruno Brunelli, who can usually conjure up impossible tickets or reservations. While its overall appearance isn't quite as glitzy as that of some other hotels in this price category, the Mayfair more than makes up for its slightly lived-in feel (which many guests, incidentally, prefer) with friendliness and an always-lively atmosphere. ☎ *610 Park Ave., 10021,* ☎ *212/288–0800 or 800/545–4000,* FAX *201/737–0538. 150 rooms. Restaurant, lobby lounge, meeting rooms. AE, DC, MC, V.*

★ **The Peninsula.** The former Gotham Hotel on 5th Avenue now belongs to the respected Peninsula Group whose Hong Kong flagship consistently gets top ratings. Most of the guest rooms are of a generous size, deep-carpeted, and soberly furnished. They're matched by sumptuous (by New York or any standards) marble baths with bidets, outsize tubs (many of them Jacuzzis), and collectible, bergamot-scented Lanvin goodies. Even the smaller rooms have graceful sculpted Art Nouveau–style headboards, desks, and armoires; some also have the same sweeping views down 5th Avenue as the more expensive suites. The rooftop health club, with state-of-the-art exercise machines, a decent-size pool, massage and facial services, and a dining area with a terrace, is a knockout. ☎ *700 5th Ave., 10019,* ☎ *212/ 247–2200 or 800/262–9467,* 𝔽𝔸𝕏 *212/903–3949. 250 rooms. Restaurant, café, lobby lounge, pool, health club, meeting rooms. AE, DC, MC, V.*

The Plaza. Occupying the entire southwest corner of Central Park West and 5th Avenue, with its front-yard fountain and unsurpassed location opposite Central Park and F.A.O. Schwarz, the Plaza is probably the most high-profile of all New York hotels. Donald Trump bought it (in 1988), the fictional Eloise ran riot in it (and her "portrait" adorns the Palm Court), and film upon film has featured it—from *North by Northwest* in the 1950s and *Breakfast at Tiffany's* and *Barefoot in the Park* in the 1960s, through the 1971 *Plaza Suite,* and the more recent *Sleepless in Seattle, Scent of a Woman,* and *Home Alone 2.* And does the institution live up to the hype? Reports are good. Furnishings, though still hotel-like in most units, are of high quality. Bathrooms have fluffy new towels and toiletries. One real advantage here is the size of guest rooms—only a handful of other classic properties can offer similar spaciousness in nearly all accommodations. One thing's for sure: Even if it's your first time in New York, a quick nip at the dimly lit Oak Bar or a stroll by the fin-de-siècle Palm Court will make you feel part of what makes the city tick. ☎ *5th Ave. at 59th St., 10019,* ☎ *212/759–3000 or 800/228– 3000,* 𝔽𝔸𝕏 *212/546–5324. 807 rooms. 2 restaurants, 2 bars, café, meeting rooms. AE, DC, MC, V.*

$$$

★ **Doral Court, Doral Park Avenue,** and **Doral Tuscany.** These three sisters are not only near neighbors in off-the-tourist-map, peaceful Murray Hill, but they keep in touch with each other, allowing guests of each to sign for food and drinks at the others' facilities. Which to choose? All have been carefully injected with the feel of a small European hotel: The Park Avenue has amusing neoclassical follies mixed in with 20s Deco, while the other two are more sober, in a wood-paneled, country house way. The Tuscany is the priciest, the $20–$30 extra reflected in the rooms' Italian marble bathrooms, separate dressing areas with sink, walk-in closets, entrance halls, and three phones. Next is the Court, where you live without the marble and get dressed in a mere alcove, then the Park Avenue is the bargain, where you lack the space for a dressing area, but your bathroom is marble. ☎ *Doral Court, 130 E. 39th St., 10016,* ☎ *212/685–1100 or 800/223–6725,* ☒ *212/779–0148. 199 rooms. Doral Park Avenue, 70 Park Ave., at 38th St., 10016,* ☎ *212/687– 7050 or 800/223–6725,* ☒ *212/779–0148. 202 rooms. Doral Tuscany, 120 E. 39th St., 10016,* ☎ *212/686–1600 or 800/223–6725,* ☒ *212/779–0148. 121 rooms. Combined 4 restaurants, 2 bars, health club, meeting rooms.*

The Michelangelo. The Theater District's only true deluxe hotel, having been through several incarnations, most recently as the Parc 51 and the Grand Bay, seems to have settled happily with the Italian Starhotels company, and is better and friendlier than in the past. The rooms are bigger than they need be, and have either French country decor or a distinctly deco feel (curvy black lacquered or pale oak closets concealing TVs, or fitted bar areas in the larger rooms; much chrome and glass). All have king-size beds, multiline phones, and fine—Italian, of course—marble bathrooms with bidets, TVs, and phones. The staff is helpful, with a concierge who is a cut above the usual found in New York City hotels. ☎ *152 W. 51st St., 10019,* ☎ *212/765–1900 or 800/237–0990,* ☒ *212/581–7618. 178 rooms. Restaurant, bar, lobby lounge, exercise room, meeting rooms. AE, DC, MC, V.*

The New York Palace. This glass monolith with a landmark palazzo at its feet is many visitors' vision of the ideal New York hotel: big, slightly overwrought, and always busy. Palace rooms are generous by Manhattan standards; those on the higher floors enjoy views of St. Patrick's Cathedral and the East Side from windows which, rather worryingly, open wide at the bottom. In your room, you may find the minibar empty, and no robe or in-room safe, but, you will find such extravagant amenities as Caswell-Massey toiletries, an iron, *and* a shoe-polishing machine. Public rooms, many of them located in the 100-year-old Villard Houses at the hotel's base, contain valuable pieces of art and lovely architectural details, and there are a variety of bars and eating spots. The staff is friendly, if occasionally harried. ☎

455 Madison Ave., 10022, ☎ 212/888–7000 or 800/221–4982, ℻ 212/355–0820. 963 rooms. Restaurant, 2 bars, 2 lobby lounges, tea shop, kitchenettes, meeting rooms. AE, DC, MC, V.

★ **The Royalton.** As hip today as it was when it opened its steel-and-glass doors to the '80s, Ian Schrager and the late Steve Rubell's second Manhattan hotel (Morgan's came first) is a second home to the world's media, music, and fashion biz folk. Even someone who has never opened a copy of *Vogue* (whose editors hang out here) can't fail to be thunderstruck by the difference between this and traditional-style hotels like, say, the Algonquin across the street. French designer Philippe Starck—he of the pointy-ended toothbrush and the chrome lemon squeezer on stilts—transformed spaces of intimidating size into a paradise for poseurs, with vividly colored, geometrically challenged but comfy chairs and couches and lots of catwalk-style gliding areas. Rooms, suffice it to say, are just as glamorously offbeat, some of them oddly shaped and none too big, but all of them perfectly comfortable, especially with the service you get here, which caters to people who feel it's their lot in life to be waited on. ⊞ *44 W. 44th St., 10036, ☎ 212/869–4400 or 800/635–9013, ℻ 212/869–8965. 205 rooms. Restaurant, bar, lobby lounge, exercise room, library, meeting rooms. AE, DC, MC, V.*

The Waldorf-Astoria. Along with the Plaza (*see above*), this Art Deco masterpiece personifies New York at its most lavish and powerful. Hilton, its owner, spent a fortune on refurbishing both public areas and guest rooms a couple of years ago, and the bloom hasn't faded yet, from the original murals and mosaics and elaborate plaster ornamentation to the fine old-wood walls and doors. In the guest rooms, some of which start at the low end of this category, there are new bedspreads, carpets, and other signs of upgrading. Bathrooms throughout are old but beautifully kept up and rather spacious. Of course, in the very private Tower section, everything becomes just that much grander. You can eat an ur-Waldorf salad at Peacock Alley then work it off with a personal trainer at the Plus One fitness center. The hotel's richly tinted, hushed lobby serves as an interior centerpoint of city life. ⊞ *301 Park Ave., 10022, ☎ 212/355–3000 or 800/HILTONS, ℻ 212/421–8103. 1,692* *rooms. 3 restaurants, coffee shop, lobby lounge, tea shop, exercise room, meeting rooms. AE, DC, MC, V.*

$$

The Algonquin. While this landmark property's English-drawing-room atmosphere and burnished-wood lobby have been kept mercifully intact, its working parts (the plumbing, for instance) and bedrooms have been renovated. This much-beloved hotel, where the Round Table group of writers and wits once met for lunch, still shelters celebrities, particularly literary types visiting nearby publishing houses or the *New Yorker* magazine offices. Late-night performances go on as usual at the Oak Room. Bathrooms and sleeping quarters retain Victorian-style fixtures and furnishings, only now there are larger, firmer beds, modern TVs, VCRs (upon request), computerized phones, and Caswell-Massey toiletries. Tubs, tiles, and sinks are still—some say quaintly—old-fashioned. ☎ *59 W. 44th St., 10036,* ☎ *212/840–6800 or 800/548–0345,* ℻ *212/944–1419. 165 rooms. Restaurant, 2 lobby lounges, business services, meeting rooms, free parking on weekends. AE, DC, MC, V.*

★ **The Fitzpatrick.** This cozy Irish "boutique" hotel is conveniently situated just south of Bloomingdale's and seconds away from anchor bus and subway routes. Nearly half of the 92 units are true suites that are priced well below the market average, even on weekdays. Amenities include trouser presses, telephones with voice mail, and subdued traditional furnishings. Though not especially large, bathrooms are modern and well equipped; most come with whirlpools. A small restaurant called Fitzers features Irish seafood in season and a lively bar, which has become popular with locals. The staff is exceptionally friendly and savvy, which may be why celebs such as Gregory Peck and Stephen Rea are checking in. ☎ *687 Lexington Ave., 10022,* ☎ *212/355–0100 or 800/367–7701,* ℻ *212/308–5166. 92 rooms. Restaurant, bar, meeting room. AE, DC, MC, V.*

Manhattan East Suite Hotels. Here's a group of good-value properties for the traveler who likes to combine full hotel service with independent pied-à-terre living. These nine midtown hotels have different characters and varying prices, though all have been edging up and nearly all now top the

$$ category in busy seasons. The five best are the **Beekman Tower** (3 Mitchell Pl.), near the United Nations; the **Dumont Plaza** (150 E. 34th St.); the **Surrey Hotel** (20 E. 76th St.), in the neighborhood of Madison Avenue art galleries and designer boutiques; the **Southgate Tower** (371 7th Ave.), an attractive and secure place to sleep near Madison Square Garden and Penn Station, with the lowest rates of the bunch; and the **Eastgate Tower** (222 E. 39th St.), with the second-lowest rates. Except for the modern style at the Dumont, all have traditional guest-room decor; the Surrey's rooms border on the truly elegant. Most accommodations have pantries, and larger units have dining areas with full-size tables. The older hotels in the group do have some disappointing rooms, but overall these properties are outstanding for convenience, location, and space. ⌨ *Sales office, 500 W. 37th St., 10018,* ☎ *212/465–3600 or 800/ME–SUITE,* 🖷 *212/465–3663. AE, DC, MC, V.*

★ **Mayflower.** Step under the green awning into the long, low, wood-paneled lobby, with its leather chesterfields, plants in oriental pots, and gilt-framed oils of tall ships and flowers, take an apple from the basket on the registration desk, and you feel truly welcomed to New York—such is the charm of this venerable hotel on Central Park. Rooms are very spacious for midtown, and most include walk-in pantries with a fridge and sink; invest an extra $20 for a high-up front room, and you get the only-in-New-York bonus of a heartbreakingly spectacular park view. The most recently refurbished rooms feature carpets so thick they bounce, with fruit-and-flower-print drapes and Regency striped upholstery, dark wood colonial furniture, and pinky-beige tiled bathrooms. In summertime everyone wants the private wraparound terrace of the five penthouse suites (at $300–$400). ⌨ *15 Central Park West, 10023,* ☎ *212/265–0060 or 800/223–4164,* 🖷 *212/265–2026. 577 rooms. Restaurant, bar, exercise room. AE, D, DC, MC, V.*

★ **Morgans.** Until recently, the first hotel in nightclub mavens Ian Schrager and the late Steve Rubell's triumphant triumvirate was so discreet, it eschewed publicity of all kinds, but now it doesn't mind if you manage to find it. There's no sign outside or in the monochrome lobby to assist you, which, for many of the guests, some of them famous, is a definite turn-on. Yes, from the speckled beige-gray-white walls to the cushions on the windowseat, from the built-in-closet doors to the specially commissioned Mapplethorpe photographs, everything is pretty much in shades that jump between black and white. Exquisite, tiny bathrooms have checkered tile stripes like on the old cabs, crystal glass doors on the shower, brushed steel sinks, and snob-value Kiehl's toiletries. There are vague plans afoot to add a restaurant, but for now, there's only a laid-back breakfast room with a complimentary buffet. If you care deeply about style, can't afford the Royalton, or don't want to be on show, there is no better place to stay in New York. ☎ *237 Madison Ave., 10016, ☎ 212/686–0300, FAX 212/779–8352. 112 rooms. Breakfast room. AE, DC, MC, V.*

Radisson Empire Hotel. A change in ownership transformed this old place into a useful and reliable option. The English country–style lobby is warm and inviting; halls are decorated in soft gray with elegant lamps. Rooms and suites are a bit like small boxes, but nicely furnished; special room features include high-tech electronics, and the small but immaculate baths have heated towel racks. There is a cozy "British" lounge on the second floor that New Yorkers in the know have discovered. Although this hotel's prices have gone up, it's still one of the city's better buys in terms of quality and location, right across the street from Lincoln Center. ☎ *Broadway at 63rd St., 10023, ☎ 212/265–7400, 800/221–6509, or 800/223–9868, FAX 212/315–0349. 368 rooms. Restaurant. AE, DC, MC, V.*

★ **The Shoreham.** "But darling, Lucretia *always* stays at the Shoreham. Yes, I know it's only a year old. She used to stay at the *Franklin*—it's run by the same people but it's on the Upper East, darling, and it's too full of models. The *Shoreham's* got that angelic lounge with the car seats and crackled glass and tulips and British and Italian *Vogues.*" Enough of that. This is a miniature Royalton with less attitude and more peace, but almost as much visual frippery, albeit sober of hue and comfortable to boot. Almost everything is metal, from a perforated steel table, lit from within and draped in see-through gold organza, to the steel sink and matching beaker in the shiny, tiny bathrooms. Things that aren't actually metal are metal-colored, like the silver gray carpets and black oval nighttables, with digital gadgetry and—nice touch—a single red rose. There's much to control remotely: TV, VCR, CD are in all rooms, with a complimentary library of sounds and movies. And, darling, those cedar-lined closets are to *die for.* ☎ *33 W 55th St, 10019,* ☎ *212/247–6700,* ℻ *212/765–9741. 84 rooms. Lobby lounge. AE, DC, MC, V.*

The Warwick. Well placed for theater and points west, this handsome and cozy classic belonging to a Geneva-based chain recently finished a major overhaul—or so it should have by now, though you may wish to double check in case any of the '70s nightmare rooms with giant bamboo-print wallpaper still remain. The new decor is the familiar, comforting hotel version of Regency style, with hardwood furniture, smooth, thick carpets, and floral drapes. The lobby-lounge is most inviting, with a dark green bar and the huge Tudor murals of the Ciao Europa restaurant on either side of the entrance, lots of armchairs, and marble floors. ☎ *65 W. 54th St.,* ☎ *212/247–2700,* ℻ *212/957– 8915. 425 rooms. Restaurant, bar, lobby lounge, meeting rooms. AE, DC, MC, V.*

$

Ameritania. This converted single-room-occupancy hotel is a pleasant choice for the theatergoer or business traveler with an eye on the bottom line, especially since a lot of updating was completed only recently, ensuring that everything from the lobby to the simple rooms is modern and cheerful. Some units have superior baths and amenities. The hotel's proximity to Broadway hits and popular night spots such as the Ritz should keep the clientele on the youthful side. ☎ *1701 Broadway, 10019,* ☎ *212/247–5000,* ℻ *212/ 247–3316. 250 rooms. Restaurant, lobby lounge, exercise room. AE, DC, MC, V.*

The Barbizon. Three blocks from Bloomingdale's is this 22-story tawny brick neo-Gothic hotel, famous until the mid-70s as the Barbizon Hotel for Women, where Grace Kelly and Candice Bergen, among others, rested unmolested in the library or tea lounge. Refurbishment all but halved the room total (to 300) and doubled the size of most, but try for one of the still-small studio rooms, of which there are some 35: at under $100 a night, they're a great deal for the neighborhood. These rooms come with the same facilities as the more expensive rooms and suites (which are nothing special)—in-house movies on TV, individual air-conditioning control and phone. 🖾 *140 E. 63rd St., 10021,* ☎ *212/838–5700,* 🖷 *212/753–0360. 345 rooms with bath. Restaurant, bar, meeting rooms. AE, DC, MC, V.*

★ **Beacon.** Three blocks from Central Park, or the same from Lincoln Center, this exquisite little hotel lays on many features it needn't have bothered with, but did anyway. In the large standard rooms—as in the suites—are kitchenettes with full-size fridge-freezers and four-ring stoves (so you can take advantage of Zabar's down the block); the closets are huge, the dark wood furniture elegantly new, the bathrooms complete with hairdryers and lit with Hollywood dressing room bulbs. You get voice mail on your phone, of which there are two in the suites (which, at $30 extra, only just bust the **$** category), as well as two TVs. With so much in the neighborhood, it's no drawback that there's no restaurant or bar; neither does it matter that the only lounge is the tony gold-ceilinged, black-and-white marble floored lobby—not when the rooms are this comfortable. 🖾 *2130 Broadway, at 75th St, 10023,* ☎ *212/787–1100 or 800/572–4969,* 🖷 *212/724–0839. 160 rooms. AE, DC, MC, V.*

★ **Gramercy Park.** The terra-cotta-color, Queen Anne–style hotel is almost the only one in this elegant neighborhood, which boasts the city's least-populated park. The park remains thus because it's locked, but hotel guests can use it. Further advantages to staying here include more peace and quiet than is usual, and a bar straight out of a Cole Porter lyric, with pianist, hot hors d'oeuvres, and wicked martinis. A favorite of British actors and TV people, for some reason, the Gramercy is also particularly friendly, with staff who have spent their careers here. Don't expect too much from the rooms, but they are mostly way above average for this price range. 🖾 *2 Lexington Ave., 10010,* ☎ *212/475–4320,* 🖷 *212/505–0535. 180 rooms. Bar, lobby lounge. AE, D, DC, MC, V.*

Jolly Madison Towers. Who could resist that name? Actually, it refers not to the ambience but to the Italian chain that took this place off Best Western's hands about three years ago and proceeded with an overdue remodeling. For this safe and tony neighborhood, prices are reasonable, especially since decor, service, and facilities are unobjectionable, if unspectacular. Rooms are small but handsome in deep sapphire and dove gray, with dark wood headboards and desks; king-size beds in the superiors, queen-size elsewhere. Bathrooms are tiny, with marbleized vanities and white tiles around compact tubs. ⊞ *22 E. 38th St., 10016,* ☎ *212/685–3700,* ℻ *212/447–0747. 225 rooms. Bar, coffee shop, health club. AE, DC, MC, V.*

★ **Paramount.** What used to be the dowdy Century Paramount was completely transformed by the same team that owns the Royalton (*see above*), and Morgans (*see above*), into a cut-rate version of the same, so irresistible it's nearly always full. In the Phillippe Starck lobby, a cliff of concrete and glamorous sweep of staircase lead to a mezzanine gallery of squashy seating and tiny nightclub-style table lamps for dining and spying on the glitterati below, a separate bar, and a hilarious children's playroom. Despite appearances, the staff is most welcoming, and there's a perennial scene in the other bar off the lobby, which remains packed into the wee hours. Rumors that the bedrooms are minute are true. They make up for it with wacky touches, like lights that reproduce the look of dappled sunlight, zebra-striped headboards, and conical steel sinks in the bathrooms—all bearing the Starck stamp—and VCRs as standard issue. There's a Dean & DeLuca takeout off the lobby, plus a fitness center. For the forever young and arty, it's the best place. ⊞ *235 W. 46th St., 10036,* ☎ *212/764–5500 or 800/225–7474,* ℻ *212/354–5237. 610 rooms. 2 restaurants, bar, exercise room, business services. AE, DC, MC, V.*

Park Savoy. Follow the mirrored tunnel with diagonal stripes of ridged aluminum directly opposite the Essex House's 58th Street entrance and you'll find the Park Savoy's all-purpose registration, information, concierge, and switchboard desk. Of course there's no bellhop, no room service, no direct dial phone, no cable channels on the ancient TV, but for a room costing under $40 way up to $79, from which you can smell Central Park, hear Carnegie Hall, and taste the caviar at Petrossian and the Russian Tea Room, who's counting? To talk about the "decor" of the rooms would be a stretch: William Morris drapes, wine colored carpet, rock hard beds, a print of a little girl in a daisy field, peeling paint—these convey the style. There are, however, fridges

in about 20 rooms, and kitchenettes in ten, adequate closets, no mildew in the bathrooms, and a little more space than
some chain hotels at twice the price. Also, the staff (OK, the
guy behind the desk) knows all the guests—there's a lot of
repeat business, including many families, which makes for
a safe feeling. 🖬 *158 W. 58th St, 10019,* ☎ *212/245–5755,*
🅵🅰🆇 *212/765–0668. 96 rooms. AE, MC, V.*

Pickwick Arms Hotel. This convenient East Side establishment charges $85 a night for standard renovated doubles
but has older singles with shared baths for as little as $40.
The marble-clad lobby is chandeliered, and often cozily
bustling, since this place is routinely booked solid by bargain hunters. Privations you endure in order to save a buck
really start and end with the postage-stamp size of the
room, unless you're sensitive about interior design. All
rooms are different, maybe bamboo-furnished, possibly
painted yellow, but certainly not photogenic. However, the
place is well-run, and it's safe, and some windows look over
the Manhattan skyline the same way they do at the Plaza.
🖬 *230 E. 51st St., 10022,* ☎ *212/355–0300 or 800/742–
9425,* 🅵🅰🆇 *212/755–5029. 400 rooms. AE, MC, V.*

Washington Square Hotel. This cozy hotel has a true European feel and style, from the wrought-iron and brass
in the small but elegant lobby to the personal attention
given by the staff. Rooms and baths are simple but pleasant and recently renovated, not that you'll spend much
time in them, with so many shopping, eating, and drinking opportunities on the doorstep. Complimentary continental breakfast is included in the room rate. The manager
has strong ties to the local jazz community and can provide tips if you want to catch a set at the nearby Blue Note,
or one of the other famous clubs around here. 🖬 *103 Waverly Pl., 10011,* ☎ *212/777–9515 or 800/222–0418,* 🅵🅰🆇
*212/979–8373. 160 rooms. Restaurant, laundry service.
AE, DC, MC, V.*

6 The Arts and Nightlife

THE ARTS

Updated
by David
Low

IN NEW YORK, the arts routinely make the headlines. Pick up a week's worth of newspapers and you'll learn of casting disputes at the Metropolitan Opera, prima ballerinas with bruised knees, big Broadway musicals whose directors are replaced hours before opening, and the constant entertaining haggles among backers, artists, and critics. It's chaos. What a town!

Much has been made of the ballooning cost of tickets, especially for Broadway shows—though major concerts and recitals don't come cheap in New York, either. The top Broadway ticket prices for musicals are $75; the best seats for nonmusicals usually cost $55, although they occasionally hit the $65 mark.

On the positive side, tickets for New York City's arts events aren't hard to come by—unless, of course, you're dead set on seeing the season's hottest, sold-out show. Generally, a theater or concert hall's box office is the best place to buy tickets, since in-house ticket sellers make it their business to know about their theaters and shows and don't mind pointing out (on a chart) where you'll be seated. It's always a good idea to purchase tickets in advance to avoid disappointment, especially if you're traveling a long distance. For advance purchase, send the theater or hall a certified check or money order, several alternate dates, and a self-addressed stamped envelope.

You can also pull out a credit card and call **Tele-Charge** (☎ 212/239–6200) or **Ticketmaster** (☎ 212/307–4100 for Broadway and Off-Broadway shows, 212/307–7171 for other events) to reserve tickets—newspaper ads generally will specify which you should use for any given event. A surcharge (about $6) will be added per ticket, and your tickets will be waiting for you at the theater. You may be tempted to buy from the ticket scalpers who frequently haunt the lobbies of hit shows. But beware: They have reportedly sold tickets to the big hits for up to $200, when seats were still available at the box office for much less. (Also bear in mind that ticket scalping is against the law in New York.)

Off- and Off-Off-Broadway theaters have their own joint box office called **Ticket Central** (416 W. 42nd St., ☎ 212/279–4200). While there are no discounts here, tickets to performances in these theaters are less expensive than Broadway tickets—Ticket Central prices average $10–$40 per person—and they cover an array of events, including legitimate theater, performance art, and dance.

Discount Tickets

New York's best-known discount source is the **TKTS booth** in Duffy Square (47th St. and Broadway, ☎ 212/768–1818). TKTS sells day-of-performance tickets for Broadway and some Off-Broadway plays at discounts that, depending on a show's popularity, often go as low as half price (plus a $2.50 surcharge per ticket). The names of shows available on that day are posted on electronic boards in front of the booth. If you're interested in a Wednesday or Saturday matinee, go to the booth between 10 and 2, check out what's offered, and then wait in line. For evening performances, the booth is open 3–8; for Sunday matinee and evening performances, noon–8. One caution: TKTS accepts only cash or traveler's checks—no credit cards. So successful has TKTS proved that an auxiliary booth operates in the Wall Street area (2 World Trade Center mezzanine). The World Trade Center Branch is open weekdays 11–5:30, Saturday 11–3:30; for matinees and Sundays, 11–closing the day before the performance. The lines at the downtown TKTS booth are usually shorter than those at Duffy Square, though occasionally the offerings are somewhat limited.

Finding Out What's On

To find out who or what's playing where, your first stop should be the newsstand. The **New York Times** isn't a prerequisite for finding out what's going on around town, but it comes in pretty handy, especially on Friday with its "Weekend" section; the Sunday "Arts and Leisure" section features longer "think pieces" on everything from opera to TV—and a lot more ads, plus a full, detailed calendar of cultural events for the upcoming week.

If your tastes are more adventurous, try the weekly paper **The Village Voice;** its club listings are unrivaled, its "Choices" section reliable. When its club-tattler critic Michael Musto talks (in a column called "La Dolce Musto"), night prowlers and club crawlers listen. The *Voice* is published on Wednesday.

Some of the most entertaining listings can be found in the **New Yorker** magazine. "Goings On About Town" heads off each weekly issue with ruthlessly succinct reviews of theater, dance, art, music, film, and nightlife. **New York** magazine's "Cue listings" are also very useful. **Theater Week** contains up-to-date news on theater happenings all over town. The **New York Native, Christopher Street,** and **HomoExtra** cover the gay scene.

Theater

Broadway Theater District

To most people, New York theater means Broadway, that region bounded by 42nd and 53rd streets, between 6th and 9th avenues, where bright, transforming lights shine upon porn theaters and jewel-box playhouses alike.

Some of the old playhouses are as interesting for their history as for their current offerings: the **St. James** (246 W. 44th St.) is where Lauren Bacall served as an usherette in the '40s, and a sleeper of a musical called *Oklahoma!* woke up as a hit; the **Lyceum** (149 W. 45th St.) is New York's oldest still-functioning theater, built in 1903 with a posh apartment on top that now holds the Shubert Archive (open to scholars by appointment only); the **Shubert Theatre** (225 W. 44th St.) is where Barbra Streisand made her 1962 Broadway debut, and the long-run record-breaker, *A Chorus Line,* played for 15 years; and the **Martin Beck Theatre** (302 W. 45th St.), built in 1924 in Byzantine style, is the stage that served up premieres of Eugene O'Neill's *The Iceman Cometh,* Arthur Miller's *The Crucible,* and Tennessee Williams's *Sweet Bird of Youth.* Theater names read like a roll-call of American theater history: **Booth, Ethel Barrymore, Eugene O'Neill, Gershwin, Lunt-Fontanne, Richard Rodgers,** and **Neil Simon,** among others. 8:00

In determining which Broadway show to see, first consider the long-running hits: *Cats, Crazy for You, Les Misérables, The Phantom of the Opera, Miss Saigon, Sunset Boulevard,* and others, which most magazine and newspaper listings helpfully point out. Then look beyond the marquees for both tomorrow's hits and today's resounding flops. Remember, there's something special about catching a show in previews or seeing a harshly reviewed play before it bites the dust. A lousy review can quickly close a show, even though discriminating audience members often disagree with the critics.

Beyond Broadway

Ten years ago it was relatively simple to categorize the New York stage beyond Broadway. It was divided into Off-Broadway and Off-Off-Broadway, depending on a variety of factors that included theatrical contract type, location, and ticket price. Today such distinctions seem strained, as Off-Broadway prices have risen and the quality of some Off-Off-Broadway productions has improved markedly.

Name actors appear in top-flight productions at **Lincoln Center's** two theaters: the **Vivian Beaumont** and the more intimate **Mitzi E. Newhouse** (65th St. and Broadway, ☎ for both 212/362–7600), which has scored some startling successes, including John Guare's *Six Degrees of Separation,* Wendy Wasserstein's *The Sisters Rosensweig,* and an acclaimed revival of *Carousel.* Downtown at the **Joseph Papp Public Theater** (425 Lafayette St., ☎ 212/598–7150), renamed in 1992 to honor its late founder and long-time guiding genius, producer George C. Wolfe continues the tradition of innovative theater, mounting new and classic plays, along with film series, dance concerts, literary readings, and musical events. In the summertime, the Public's **Shakespeare Festival** (☎ 212/260–2400) raises its sets in Central Park's open-air **Delacorte Theater.** You can pick up free tickets on the same day of the performance beginning at 1 PM at the Delacorte Theater (mid-park, enter at W. 81st St. or E. 79th St.) or between 1 PM and 3 PM at the Public Theater box office (425 Lafayette/Astor Place).

Music

Lincoln Center (W. 62nd St. and Broadway) remains the city's musical nerve center, especially when it comes to the classics. The **New York Philharmonic,** led by Music Director

Kurt Masur, performs at **Avery Fisher Hall** (☎ 212/875–5030) late September to early June.

Near Avery Fisher is **Alice Tully Hall** (☎ 212/875–5050), an intimate "little white box," considered as acoustically perfect as concert houses get. Here the **Chamber Music Society of Lincoln Center** tunes up, along with promising Juilliard students, chamber music ensembles such as the Guarneri Quartet and Kronos Quartet, music on period instruments, choral music, famous soloists, and concert groups. Lincoln Center's outdoor Damrosch Park, and **Bruno Walter Auditorium** (in the Library of the Performing Arts, ☎ 212/870–1630) often offer free concerts. In 1996, Lincoln Center inaugurates a new summer international performance festival under the direction of arts critic and writer John Rockwell. The program includes classical music concerts, contemporary music and dance presentations, stage works, and non-Western arts.

While Lincoln Center is only 30 years old, another famous classical music palace—**Carnegie Hall** (W. 57th St. at 7th Ave., ☎ 212/247–7800)—recently celebrated its 100th birthday. This is the place where the great pianist Paderewski was attacked by ebullient crowds (who claimed kisses and locks of his hair) after a performance in 1891; where young Leonard Bernstein, standing in for New York Philharmonic conductor Bruno Walter, made his triumphant debut in 1943; where Jack Benny and Isaac Stern fiddled together; and where the Beatles played one of their first U.S. concerts. When threats of the wrecker's ball loomed large in 1960, a consortium of Carnegie loyalists (headed by Isaac Stern) rose to save it; an eventual multimillion-dollar renovation in 1986 worked cosmetic wonders.

What follows is a list of other prime classical music locales around the city:

Bargemusic at the Fulton Ferry Landing in Brooklyn (☎ 718/624–4061) keeps chamber-music groups busy year-round on an old barge with a fabulous skyline view.
Grace Rainey Rogers Auditorium at the Metropolitan Museum of Art (5th Ave. at 82nd St., ☎ 212/570–3949) offers performances of classical music in classic surroundings.

Merkin Concert Hall at the Abraham Goodman House (129 W. 67th St., ☎ 212/362–8719) is almost as prestigious as the concert halls at Lincoln Center.

Miller Theatre (Columbia University, Broadway at 116th St., 212/854–7799) features a varied program of classical performers, such as the New York Virtuosi Chamber Symphony.

Sylvia and Danny Kaye Playhouse (Hunter College, 68th St., between Park and Lexington Aves., ☎ 212/772–4448) presents a varied program of events, including distinguished soloists and chamber music groups, in a small state-of-the-art concert hall.

Opera

Recent decades have sharply intensified the public's appreciation for grand opera—partly because of the charismatic personalities of such great singers as Luciano Pavarotti, Placido Domingo, and Cecilia Bartoli, and partly because of the efforts of New York's magnetic Metropolitan Opera. A Met premiere draws the rich and famous, the critics, and the connoisseurs. At the Met's elegant Lincoln Center home, with its Marc Chagall murals and weighty Austrian-crystal chandeliers, the supercharged atmosphere gives audiences a sense that something special is going to happen, even before the curtain goes up. Luciano Pavarotti put it best: "When it comes to classical music, New York can truly be called a beacon of light—with that special quality that makes it *unico in mondo,* unique in the world."

The **Metropolitan Opera** (☎ 212/362–6000) performs its vaunted repertoire from October to mid-April, and though tickets can cost more than $100, many less expensive seats and standing room are available. The top-priced tickets are the center box seats, which are actually few in number and almost never available without a subscription. Standing room tickets for the week's performance go on sale on Saturday.

The **New York City Opera,** which performs from September through November and in March and April at Lincoln Center's New York State Theater (212/870–5570) continues its tradition of offering a diverse repertoire consisting of adventurous and rarely seen works as well as beloved classic opera and operetta favorites. The company maintains its ingenious practice of "supertitling"—electronically displaying above the stage, line-by-line English translation of foreign-language operas. Recent seasons have included such old favorites as *Carmen, Madama Butterfly,* and *La Traviata* as well as premieres of challenging new works such as *The Times of Harvey Milk.*

Opera aficionados should also keep track of the **Carnegie Hall** schedule (☎ 212/247–7800) for debuting singers and performances by the Opera Orchestra of New York, which specializes in presenting rarely performed operas in concert form, often with star soloists.

Dance

Ballet

The **New York City Ballet,** a hallmark troupe for nearly 50 years, recently celebrated its 100th season with compelling examples of exceptional dances created by the Company's Master-in-Chief, Peter Martins. The company's vast repertory also includes works by George Balanchine, Jerome Robbins, and others. NYCB performs in Lincoln Center's New York State Theater (☎ 212/870–5570). Its winter season runs from mid-November through February—with the beloved annual production of Balanchine's *The Nutcracker* ushering in the December holiday season—while its spring season lasts from mid-April through June.

Across the plaza at Lincoln Center, the Metropolitan Opera House (☎ 212/362–6000) is home to **American Ballet Theatre,** renowned for its brilliant renditions of the great 19th-century classics (*Swan Lake, Giselle, The Sleeping Beauty,* and *The Nutcracker*), as well as for the unique scope of its eclectic contemporary repertoire (including works by all the 20th-century masters—Balanchine, Tudor, Robbins, and de Mille, among others). Since its inception in 1940, the Company has included some of the greatest dancers of the century, such as Mikhail Baryshnikov, Natalia Makarova, Rudolf Nureyev, Gelsey Kirkland, and Cynthia Gregory. Its New York season runs from April to June.

Part of Lincoln Center's dance vitality is accounted for by the presence of the **School of American Ballet,** the focus for the dreams of young dancers across the country. You can see SAB students dashing across 66th and Broadway with leotard-stuffed bags slung over their shoulders, or congregating in **The Ballet Shop** (1887 Broadway, between 62nd and 63rd Sts., ☎ 212/581–7990).

Modern Dance

A growing international modern dance center is the **Joyce Theater** (175 8th Ave., ☎ 212/242–0800), housed in a former Art Deco movie theater. The Joyce is the permanent home of **Feld Ballets/NY,** founded in 1974 by an upstart ABT dancer who went on to become a principal fixture on the dance scene. Other featured companies include the **Garth Fagan Dance** company, the lyrical **Lar Lubovitch Dance Company,** the spirited **Ballet Hispanico,** and the loony acrobats of **Pilobolus.** The Joyce has an eclectic program, including tap, jazz, ballroom, and ethnic dance, and it also showcases emerging choreographers. At **Symphony Space** (2537 Broadway, ☎ 212/864–5400), the bill often features ethnic dance.

Here's a sampling of other, mostly experimental and avant-garde, dance forums:

Dance Theater Workshop (219 W. 19th St., ☎ 212/924–0077), one of New York's most successful laboratories for new dance.

DIA Center for the Arts (155 Mercer St., ☎ 212/431–9232) hosts a number of performances by interesting local dancers.

P.S. 122 (150 1st Ave., ☎ 212/477–5288), where dance events border on performance art.

TriBeCa Performing Arts Center (199 Chambers St., ☎ 212/346–8500) presents dance troupes from around the world.

Film and Video

For information on first-run movie schedules and theaters, dial 212/777–FILM, the MovieFone sponsored by WQHT 97 FM and the *New York Times.* You can also call this number to order tickets in advance with a credit card; not all movie theaters participate, however, and the surcharge is $1 per ticket.

Museums

The **American Museum of the Moving Image** (35th Ave. at 36th St., Queens, ☎ 718/784–0077) is the only U.S. museum devoted to motion pictures, video, and interactive media. Located on the site of the historic Kaufman Astoria Studios, it offers multiple galleries that are a movie buff's paradise, as are its 195-seat Riklis Theatre and 60-seat Warner Communications Screening Room. The museum presents changing exhibits and provocative film programs, including major artist-oriented retrospectives, Hollywood classics, experimental videos, and TV documentaries.

In midtown Manhattan, the **Museum of Television & Radio** (25 W. 52nd St., ☎ 212/621–6800) has a gigantic collection of 60,000 radio and TV shows, including everything from *The Dick Van Dyke Show* to *Soap, Cheers,* and *Taxi.* The museum's library provides 96 consoles where you can watch or listen to whatever you wish for up to two hours at a time. The museum presents scheduled theater screenings, gallery exhibits, and series for children.

First-Run Houses

Manhattan's most impressive multiplex movie house, **Sony Theatres Lincoln Square** (Broadway and 68th St., ☎ 212/336–5000 or 212/595–6391), opened in November 1994. This complex has 12 state-of-the-art theaters designed to recall grand old movie palaces and an eight-story, 600-seat IMAX theater that is equipped not only for large-scale formatted films but also for 3-D imagery.

Two other New York theaters preserve the size and allure of the great movie houses of the past: The **Ziegfeld** (141 W. 54th St., west of 6th Ave., ☎ 212/765–7600), with its awesome sound system, and **Radio City Music Hall** (1260 6th Ave., ☎ 212/247–4777), with its 34-foot-high screen and 4,500-watt projector, only rarely used for movie screenings.

Midnight Movies

At a handful of Greenwich Village theaters, midnight madness continues with late and late-late showings of eccentric classics such as *Blue Velvet* and *The Rocky Horror Picture Show.* The **Angelika Film Center** (W. Houston and Mercer Sts., ☎ 212/995–2000) and the **Cinema Village 12th**

Street (12th St., between 5th Ave. and University Pl., ☎ 212/924–3363) are good theaters to check out for these.

Revival Houses

One of the best places to see old films in Manhattan opened in 1991: the **Walter Reade Theater** at Lincoln Center (70 Lincoln Plaza, Broadway and 65th St., ☎ 212/875–5600), operated by the Film Society of Lincoln Center. This comfortable movie house presents several fascinating series that run concurrently, devoted to specific themes or a certain director's body of work; movies for kids are featured Saturday morning.

Revivals can also be found at **Film Forum** (209 W. Houston St., ☎ 212/727–8110), with three screens showing often quirky series based on movie genres, directors, and other film artists.

Foreign and Independent Films

Angelika 57 (225 W. 57th St., ☎ 212/586–1900), showing film programs similar to its downtown sister theater (*see below*).

Angelika Film Center (W. Houston and Mercer Sts., ☎ 212/995–2000), offering several screens devoted to offbeat independent and foreign films, as well as a lively café catering to a youthful crowd.

Carnegie Hall Cinemas (887 7th Ave., between 56th and 57th Sts., ☎ 212/265–2520), where intriguing new films find long runs.

Cinema Village 12th Street (12th St., between 5th Ave. and University Pl., ☎ 212/924–3363), offering innovative independent features and occasional animation festivals.

Eastside Playhouse (3rd Ave., between 55th and 56th Sts., ☎ 212/755–3020), with an emphasis on first-run art films.

Lincoln Plaza (Broadway, between 62nd and 63rd Sts., ☎ 212/757–2280), six subterranean cinemas playing long-run foreign hits.

Readings and Lectures

The **New York City Poetry Calendar** (60 E. 4th St., Apt. 21, 10003, ☎ 212/475–7110), published monthly, provides an extensive list of prose and poetry readings around the city.

The calendar is available by subscription and free at several Manhattan bookstores. Check also listings for readings in **New York** magazine, the **New Yorker,** and the **Village Voice.**

NIGHTLIFE

Clubs and Entertainment

By Susan
Spano
Wells

Revised by
Stephanie
Dolgoff

Okay, so you've taken the Staten Island Ferry, you've lunched at the Plaza, and you've visited the Met. But don't tuck yourself in just yet. Instead, get yourself truly attuned to the Big Apple's schedule, which runs more by New York nocturnal than by eastern standard time. Even if you're not a night owl by habit, it's worth staying up late at least once, for by night, Manhattan takes on a whole new identity.

For the tattooed and pierced, *Paper* magazine's "P.M. 'Til Dawn" and bar sections have as good a listing as exists of the roving clubs and best of the fashionable crowd's hangouts. The more staid Friday *New York Times*'s "Weekend" section carries a "Sounds Around Town" column that can clue you in to what's in the air, as can the *Village Voice,* which probably has more nightclub ads than any other rag in the world. Or stop by Tower Records (Broadway and E. 4th St., ☎ 212/505–1500; Broadway and W. 66th St., ☎ 212/799–2500), where fliers about coming events and club passes are stacked in the entry. You may also get good tips from a suitably au courant hotel concierge. Just remember that what's hot and what's not changes almost weekly in this city, so visitors are at a distinct disadvantage. We've tried to give you a rounded sample of reliable hangouts—establishments that are likely to be still in business by the time you use this book—but clubs come and go as fast as spawning tsetse flies, so phone ahead to make sure your target night spot hasn't closed or turned into a polka hall (unless, of course, the polka's your thing). Most will charge a cover of $10–$20 a head, depending on the club and the night. Take cash, because many places don't accept plastic.

Putting on the Ritz

The Ballroom (253 W. 28th St., ☎ 212/244–3005). This very hip Chelsea spot has an extensive tapas bar and a night-club where some of the great chanteuses—including Phoebe Légère and Peggy Lee—rhapsodize, and where Broadway's best moonlight after the shows or on their nights off.

The Carlyle (35 E. 76th St., ☎ 212/744–1600). The hotel's discreetly sophisticated Café Carlyle is where Bobby Short plays when he's in town; otherwise, you might find Eartha Kitt purring by a piano. Bemelman's Bar, with murals by the author of the Madeline books, regularly stars jazz pianist Barbara Carroll.

The Oak Room (at the Algonquin Hotel, 59 W. 44th St., ☎ 212/840–6800). You'll hear that the Algonquin has faded, but this room still offers yesteryear's charms. Just head straight for the long, narrow club-cum-watering hole; at the piano you'll find, perhaps, the hopelessly romantic Andrea Marcovicci or (sigh!) Harry Connick, Jr.

The Rainbow Room and **Rainbow & Stars** (30 Rockefeller Plaza, ☎ 212/632–5000). You can find two kinds of heaven high up on Rockefeller Center's 65th floor. The Rainbow Room serves dinner, and dancing to the strains of a live orchestra takes place on a floor right out of an Astaire-Rogers musical. At the intimate Rainbow & Stars, singers such as Maureen McGovern and Rosemary Clooney entertain, backlit by a view of the twinkling lights of the city.

Supper Club (240 W. 47th St., ☎ 212/921–1940). Note the last four digits of the telephone number. This huge, prix-fixe dinner-and-dancing club specializes in cheek-to-cheek Big Band sounds on Friday and Saturday nights, complete with a full orchestra. Dinner is served during the week, but call ahead to make sure you don't crash a private soirée.

Clubbing

Crane Club (408 Amsterdam Ave., ☎ 212/877–3097). A plush club with a good-looking crowd (if you can stand investment bankers) offers Top-40 hits and dinner every Thursday, Friday, and Saturday.

Delia's Supper Club (197 E. 3rd St., ☎ 212/254–9184). They serve terrific food here, but after 11 or so, the chairs are pushed back to create a tiny yet happening dance floor for the cool but not unbearably hip East Village crowd.

Expo (124 W. 43rd St., ☎ 212/819–0377). Standing where Xenon, the legendary disco, dominated in the '70s, revelers dance among decorations from the 1939 World's Fair. Spotted: Tupak Shakur, model Linda Evangelista, and Slash, among others.

Le Bar Bat (311 W. 57th St., ☎ 212/307–7228). This bamboo-encrusted, multi-tiered monster of a club fits right in with the Planet Hollywoods on 57th Street's Theme Restaurant Row, but a flashy good time can be had here among the Euro and prepster poseurs.

Limelight (47 W. 20th St., ☎ 212/807–7850). Affectionately known as "Slimelight," this transformed Chelsea church (complete with stained glass, spiral staircases, and catwalks) hosts the gamut of New York club culture, with "alternative" and heavy metal nights.

Nell's (246 W. 14th St., ☎ 212/675–1567). Back in vogue, Nell Campbell (of *Rocky Horror* fame) reintroduced sophistication to nightlife with her club. The tone in the upstairs jazz salon is Victorian; downstairs is for tête-à-têtes and dancing. The boîte opens at 10 PM and closes at 3 AM (4 AM weekends).

Sound Factory (530 W. 27th St., ☎ 212/643–0728, Saturday night only). Doors don't open until 1 AM, there's no alcohol, and usually a $15 to $20 cover, but serious dancers of all persuasions would never miss a night at the Sound Factory—and the party lasts until noon Sunday.

Supper Club (Thursday only at 240 W. 47th St., ☎ 212/921–1940) Supper's not served Thursdays so dancers can dine on the disco and funk classics. Spotted: Billy Baldwin, Mickey Rourke, and the modelesque many.

Tatou (151 E. 50th St., ☎ 212/753–1144). This pleasing addition to the supper-club scene offers dinner, dancing, and cabaret under one stylish roof. The contemporary American food goes down particularly well.

Webster Hall (125 E. 11th St., ☎ 212/353–1600). A fave among NYU students and similar species, this multistoried club has deep house on one floor, Top 40 down below, and sweaty dancers in every nook and cranny.

Jazz Notes

The Blue Note (131 W. 3rd St., ☎ 212/475–8592). This club is considered by many to be the jazz capital of the world.

Just an average week could bring Spyro Gyra, the Modern Jazz Quartet, and Joe Hendricks. Expect a steep music charge.

Bradley's (70 University Pl., ☎ 212/228–6440). With brighter-than-usual lighting and, generally, jazz piano (and sometimes a sax), this is a spot for serious fans of jazz.

Deanna's (130 E. 7th St., ☎ 212/505–5288). You won't see many familiar names at this funky East Village club, but it's cheap, casual, and the music keeps 'em coming back for more.

Fat Tuesday's (190 3rd Ave., ☎ 212/533–7902). The Les Paul Trio plays Monday in the intimate basement of this legendary spot just off Union Square.

The Knitting Factory (74 Leonard St., ☎ 212/219–3055). This eclectic gem of a cross-genre music café (recently transplanted to TriBeCa) features avant-garde jazz in a homey, funky setting. Check it out.

The Village Vanguard (178 7th Ave. S, ☎ 212/255–4037). This former Thelonius Monk haunt, the prototype of the old-world jazz club, lives on in a smoky cellar, in which jam the likes of Wynton Marsalis, among others.

Rock Your World

The Bitter End (147 Bleecker St., ☎ 212/673–7030). This old Village standby still serves up its share of new talent, as it once did Joan Armatrading and Warren Zevon. Check before arriving; blues, country, and jazz all make appearances here.

CBGB & OMFUG (315 Bowery, ☎ 212/982–4052). The full name is "Country Blue Grass Blues & Other Music For Uplifting Gourmandizers," which basically means: rock. American punk rock was born here, in this long black tunnel of a club featuring bands with inventive names: Human Remains, the Lunachicks, Iron Prostate and Who Killed Bambi?.

Don Hill's (511 Greenwich St., ☎ 212/219–2850). A TriBeCa favorite for bands both popular (Deborah Harry) and not-yet-signed (Soul Lounge). Squeeze Box parties on Friday nights are genius.

Ludlow St. Café (165 Ludlow St., ☎ (212/353–0536). In an artsy enclave just across Houston from the East Village, this basement club serves up consistently good bands.

The Mercury Lounge (217 E. Houston, ☎ 212/260–4700). With one of the best sound systems in the city, this new club in the East Village holds a quiet cachet with bands and industry insiders.

World of Music

The Anarchy Café (27 3rd Ave., ☎ 212/475–1270). Latin jazz , funk, and a Brazilian beat make this East Village spot worth a stop.

S.O.B.'s (204 Varick St., ☎ 212/243–4940). Since 1982, this has been the—and we mean *the*—place for reggae, Trinidadian carnival, zydeco, African, and especially Latin tunes. The initials stand for Sounds of Brazil, just in case you wondered. The decor is à la Tropicana; the favored drink, a Brazilian *caipirinha* (lime and Brazilian rum).

Down-Home Sounds

The Bottom Line (15 W. 4th St., ☎ 212/228–7880). Clubs come and go, but this granddaddy has stayed around since 1974. Its reputation is for showcasing talents on their way up, as it did for both Stevie Wonder and Bruce Springsteen. Recent visitors have included Buster Poindexter and Dar Williams.

Dan Lynch's Blues Bar (221 2nd Ave., ☎ 212/677–0911). This divey blues surprise in the East Village bustles with jam sessions on Saturday and Sunday afternoons.

Manny's Car Wash (1558 3rd Ave., ☎ 212/369–2583). Powerhouse blues jams on Manhattan's soul-free Upper East Side? Sounds shocking, but such is the scene every night at Manny's.

Tramps (45 W. 21st St., ☎ 212/727–7788). The place has been on the scene for two decades now, with the likes of the Dixie Dregs and NRBQ. Come here for a little Chicago blues or most any other kind of music around.

Comic Relief

Caroline's Comedy Club (1626 Broadway, between 49th and 50th Sts., ☎ 212/757–4100). This high-gloss club features established names as well as comedians on the edge of stardom. Seinfeld, Richard Jenny, and Gilbert Gottfried have all appeared.

Chicago City Limits (1105 1st Ave., tel 212/888–LAFF). This troupe's been doing improvisational comedy for a long time, and it seldom fails to whip its audiences into a laughing frenzy. Chicago City Limits performs in a renovated movie theater and is very strong on audience participation.

Freestyle Repertory Theater (various theaters, call 212/642–8202 to find out locations). Here's an improvisational theater group that's a step above the others. On one night, they may ask you to step on stage and quickly tell your life story, which five actors will then adapt into scenes; on other evenings, teams compete to outperform one another in head-to-head "theater sports matches."

Cabaret

Fez (380 Lafayette St., ☎ 212/533–2680). Tucked away in the back of the trendy Time Café, this Moroccan-themed casbah offers hilarious live soap operas, jazz, and readings amid a polished young crowd.

55 Grove Street (near Christopher St. and 7th Ave. S, ☎ 212/366–5438). You may see a Judy Garland impersonator sparring with an Ann Miller impersonator, or a mother-and-daughter team that decided all anyone needs to succeed in show business is nerve—but you'll find good entertainment as well.

Michael's Pub (211 E. 55th St., ☎ 212/758–2272). Woody Allen often moonlights on the clarinet here on Monday nights. On other evenings, other fine performers such as Mel Tormé take the stage. The crowd is very monied, very uptown.

Café Society

Bell Café (310 Spring St., ☎ 212/344–2355). An exceedingly funky but down-to-earth crowd warms this mosaic-filled TriBeCa cafe, which also offers good, cheap food.

Café Lalo (201 W. 83rd St., ☎ 212/496–6031). Pricey-but-worth-it desserts make this flashy Lautrec-themed café with its well-heeled patrons worth a taste.

Limbo (47 Ave. A, ☎ 212/477–5271). Huge pastel bowls of coffee and a chatty East Village crowd make it hard to get a table at this vaguely retro café.

Tea and Sympathy (108 Greenwich Ave., ☎ 212/807–8329). A tiny English-run tea house, complete with scones and clotted cream. It can get crowded, but it's worth the wait.

Bars

Vintage Classics

The Algonquin Hotel Lounge (59 W. 44th St., ☎ 212/840–6800). This is a venerable spot, not only because it was the site of the fabled literary Round Table, but also for its elegant tone.

Elaine's (1703 2nd Ave., ☎ 212/534–8103). The food's nothing special, and you will be relegated to an inferior table, but go to crane your neck and gawk. Woody Allen's favorite table is by the cappuccino machine. It's best to visit late, when the stars rise in Elaine's firmament.

The Four Seasons (99 E. 52nd St., ☎ 212/754–9494). Miró tapestries in the lobby greet you as you enter this power bar in the Grill Room. Watch for Kissingers and Trumps.

King Cole Bar (at the St. Regis Hotel, 2 E. 55th St., ☎ 212/753–4500). The famed Maxwell Parrish mural is a welcome sight at this gorgeous midtown rendezvous spot.

The Oak Bar (at the Plaza Hotel, 5th Ave. and 59th St., ☎ 212/759–3000). With its plummy, dark-wood furnishings, this old favorite continues to age well. Its great location draws sophisticates, shoppers, tourists in the know, and stars.

Watering Holes

SOUTH OF HOUSTON STREET

Buddha Bar (151 Varick St., tel 212/255–4433). Part owned by a French fashion photographer, this discrete yet trendy spot draws the model crowd and their oglers. Sunday is ladies' night, and Tuesdays are a must for backgammon buffs.

Ear Inn (326 Spring St., ☎ 212/226–9060). There's nothing fancy here, though it inhabits an 1817 Federal house. It's the artsy crowd that makes the place, along with Saturday-afternoon poetry readings—they call them "lunch for the ear."

Fanelli's (94 Prince St., ☎ 212/226–9412). This is a casual SoHo neighborhood bar, where many come on Sundays with the fat *New York Times* under their arms. The food's good, too.

Max Fish (Ludlow St. just below Houston, no ☎). This crowded kitsch palace on a newly artsy East Village strip boasts a twisted image of a grimacing Julio Iglesias over the bar, and a pool table in back.

Merc Bar (151 Mercer St., ☎ 212/966–2727). Once upon a time there were plans to open a classy hotel in SoHo, of which this bar was to be the cornerstone. The hotel is not to be, but the martinis here are wonderful.

Naked Lunch (17 Thompson St., ☎ 212/343–0828). Newly opened and dazzlingly successful, this Burroughs-inspired, earth-toned SoHo haunt is said to be a favorite of Eric Clapton and JFK, Jr.

CHELSEA AND THE VILLAGE

Chelsea Commons (312 10th Ave., ☎ 212/675–9233). An old-fashioned pub in front and a small tree-shaded courtyard in back, this West Chelsea bar draws a disparate but friendly crowd of bookworms, sports fans, and slackers.

Chumley's (86 Bedford St., ☎ 212/675–4449). There's no sign to help you find this place—they took it down during Chumley's speakeasy days—but when you reach the corner of Barrow Street, you're very close. A fireplace warms this relaxed spot where the burgers are hearty and the clientele collegiate.

Flower's (21 W. 17th St., ☎ 212/691–8888). This is an ultra-trendy model hangout, but you too can escape your fans in one of the cozy back-room ottomans on the roof in warm weather, overlooking the hip Photo District.

McSorley's Old Ale House (15 E. 7th St., ☎ 212/473–9148). One of New York's oldest saloons (opened in 1854), this is a must-see for first-timers to Gotham.

Peculier Pub (145 Bleecker St., ☎ 212/353–1327). Here, in the heart of the Village, you'll find 325 brands of beer, from Aass Amber to Żywiec.

The White Horse Tavern (567 Hudson St., ☎ 212/243–9260). Famous among the literati, this is the place where Dylan Thomas drained his last cup to the dregs. From April through October, there's outdoor café drinking.

EAST VILLAGE THROUGH EAST 20S

Coffee Shop (29 Union Sq. W, ☎ 212/243–7969). The models bringing you your food and drinks may not be the fastest waitpeople in the city, but a flashy, gorgeous crowd makes for an unbelievable, if attitudinal, spectacle.

Flamingo East (219 2nd Ave., ☎ 212/533–2860). Kidney-shaped sofas, style-mad patrons, moody lighting, and even moodier waiters make this haute downtown restaurant and bar a cool good time. Upstairs starts late, but the terrace overlooking the Avenue is a treat, and the food is delicious.

No-Tell Motel (167 Ave. A, no ☎). Decorated with tame 1950s porno mags, LP's, black velvet paintings of JFK and religious icons, this kitsch palace is the East Village at its most ironic.

Pete's Tavern (129 E. 18th St., ☎ 212/473–7676). This saloon is famous as the place where O. Henry wrote "The Gift of the Magi" (at the second booth to the right as you come in). These days, it's still crowded with noisy, friendly souls.

Telephone Bar (149 2nd Ave., ☎ 212/529–5000). Imported English telephone booths and a polite, handsome crowd give this pub its mark of distinction.

Temple Bar (330 Lafayette St., ☎ 212/925–4242). Romantic and pricey, this unmarked haunt is famous for its martinis and is a treat at any price.

MIDTOWN AND THE THEATER DISTRICT

Barrymore's (267 W. 45th St., ☎ 212/391–8400). This is a pleasantly downscale Theater District spot, with the requisite show posters on the wall. Listen in on the conversations at the bar and you'll hear a few tawdry, true stories of what goes on behind Broadway stage doors.

Café Un Deux Trois (123 W. 44th St., ☎ 212/354–4148). This old hotel lobby, charmingly converted, is chicly peopled. The bar itself is small, but it's a hot spot before and after the theater.

The Landmark Tavern (626 11th Ave., ☎ 212/757–8595). This aged redbrick pub (opened in 1868) is blessed by the glow of warming fireplaces on each of its three floors.

Top of the Sixes (666 5th Ave., ☎ 212/757–6662). This bar has an impressive nighttime view, whether you view St. Patrick's Cathedral to the east or Central Park to the north, from 39 stories up above 5th Avenue.

The Whiskey (at the Paramount Hotel, 235 W. 46th St., ☎ 212/764–5500). A downstairs bar graces this chic, revamped Times Square hotel that's sleek and hip, and ideal après-theater. Also fun for evening drinks is the mezzanine lounge, pure Philippe Starck-meets-the-'40s. Wear black.

EAST SIDE

P. J. Clarke's (915 3rd Ave., ☎ 212/759–1650). New York's most famous Irish bar, this establishment comes complete with the requisite mirrors and polished wood. Lots of after-workers like unwinding here, in a place that recalls the days of Tammany Hall.

The Polo Lounge (at the Westbury Hotel, 15 E. 69th St., ☎ 212/439–4835). This place is, in a word, classy; it's frequented by European royalty and Knickerbocker New York.

WEST SIDE

Chaz & Wilson's (201 W. 79th St., ☎ 212/769–0100). There must be a reason for the line out the door of this otherwise unremarkable but enduringly popular bar. Perhaps it's the live music Wednesday and Sundays, or the possibility of forging a formidable connection.

China Club (2130 Broadway, ☎ 212/877–1166). If you don't spot someone famous here within 30 minutes, you just aren't trying hard enough. Monday nights it's the place to be on the Upper West Side.

Theme Dreams

Harley Davidson Café (1370 Ave. of the Americas, ☎ 212/245–6000). Motorcycles are not allowed to park outside, which should give you an idea of the authenticity of this upholstered showroom-size restaurant. Still, rock stars and other biker fans do drop in on occasion.

Jekyll & Hyde (1409 6th Ave., ☎ 212/541–9505). "A restaurant and social club for explorers and mad scientists," Jekyll & Hyde features 250 varieties of beer and actors dressed as horror meisters who lead you through all the various scary and silly features of this multiple-story eating and ogling extravaganza. A smaller, somewhat tamer version can be found in the West Village (91 7th Ave. S, ☎ 212/966–8503).

Planet Hollywood (140 W. 57th St., ☎ 212/333–7827). It's touristy, it doesn't take reservations, and waiting lines are long. Still, the place has cachet, an undeniable star quality, and such movie memorabilia as C3PO and Dorothy's red shoes, which make up for the very compact bar.

Gay Bars

Men's Bars

Cleo's 9th Avenue Saloon (656 9th Ave., ☎ 212/307–1503). Near the Theater District, this small, narrow neighborhood bar draws a convivial, laid-back older crowd.

Crowbar (339 E. 10th St., ☏ 212/420–0670). Gay grungers and NYU students mingle happily at this East Village hot spot. Very big on Wednesday and Friday.

Stonewall (53 Christopher St., ☏ 212/463–0950). An odd mix of tourists chasing down gay history and down-to-earth locals, the scene is everything but trendy.

Ty's (114 Christopher St., ☏ 212/741–9641). Though its clientele are close-knit and fiercely loyal, this small, jeans-and-flannel neighborhood saloon never turns away friendly strangers.

The Works (428 Columbus Ave., ☏ 212/799–7365). Whether it's Thursday's $1 margarita party, or just a regular Upper West Side afternoon, the crowd is usually J. Crew–style or disco hangover.

Women's Bars

Crazy Nanny's (21 7th Ave. S, ☏ 212/366–6312). The crowd is wide-ranging—from urban chic to shaved head—and tends toward the young and wild side.

Henrietta Hudson (448 Hudson St., ☏ 212/924–3347). A little more upscale than Crazy Nanny's. The dance floor here is tiny but well utilized.

Julie's (204 E. 58th St., ☏ 212/688–1294). Popular with the sophisticated-lady, upper-crust crowd, this brownstone basement has a piano bar.

Shescapes (various locations, ☏ 212/645–6479). This roving dance party is probably the most popular of Manhattan's lesbian soirées.

INDEX